CHICAGO MAGIC

A History of STAGECRAFT & SPECTACLE

DAVID WITTER

Charleston · London

THE
History
PRESS

Published by The History Press
Charleston, SC 29403
www.historypress.net

Front cover: Copyright 1899 by the Strobridge Litho. Co., Cincinnati and New York. Library of Congress Prints and Photographs Division, Washington, D.C.

First published 2013

Manufactured in the United States

ISBN 978.1.62619.127.3

Library of Congress CIP data applied for.

CONTENTS

CONTENTS

ACKNOWLEDGEMENTS

The author would like to thank the following in order of interview or appearance: Sandy and Susan Marshall, Magic, Inc., Tom Palozzolo, Al James, Patricia Brickhouse, O'Donovan's, Sean Masterson, Eugene Burger, Gabe Fajuri, Glen C. Davies, Celeste Evans, Darby Culler, Maritess Zurbano, Jeff Taylor, the American Museum of Magic, Walter E. King, Neil Tobin, Benjamin Barnes, Magic Chicago, Dennis Watkins and Amy Witter.

INTRODUCTION

At the beginning of the twentieth century, America was on the verge of changes that would transform many aspects of everyday life and commerce. The century began with rooms largely lit by gaslights and candles; transportation by horse and train; communication by mail and telegraph; and music and entertainment provided in person by live performers in concert halls and vaudeville houses. Even photographs were a time-consuming process. During the years between 1890 and 1910, innovations like the electric light, automobile, telephone, radio, airplane and phonograph were either in the process of being invented or being honed for general use by scientists and engineers like Thomas Edison, Henry Ford, Guglielmo Marconi, Nikola Tesla, Alexander Graham Bell, the Wright brothers, George Eastman and many others. By 1930, the electric light, automobiles, telephones, phonograph records, home photography, talking pictures and the radio had become regular parts of the lives of most Americans, and air travel was on its way.

During much of this same period, Harry Houdini was breaking out of straightjackets and handcuffs; Harry Kellar was producing wine, whiskey, water and even guinea pigs from the same bottle; and Kellar and Howard Thurston were raising tables and human beings off the ground by merely gesturing with their hands. Harry Blackstone Sr. was taking what may have been the most vivid symbol of the modern age, the electric light bulb, and turning it on without any wires and then floating it through the air and out into the audience.

Blackstone's famous trick was both symbolic and ironic. The period between 1890 and 1930 has been labeled by many magic scholars as the "Golden Age of Magic." Why? It may be that, like the Romantic period in European literature, magic provided both an understanding and, more importantly, an escape from the vast technological changes that were occurring in America. Somehow, when a magician stood before an audience and made cards disappear or séance artists called forth a spirit, the past was brought back and the modern world explained. After all, it is all "magic."

During this same era, America was being transformed from a largely rural, agricultural nation to a melting pot of immigrants that became increasingly centered on cities and urban life. In no part of the country was this more true than Chicago. From 1890 to 1930, Chicago became the destination for tens of thousands of immigrants from countries ranging from first Germany and Ireland (many of whom had already settled) to Italy, Poland, Serbia, Sweden and many other European nations. Another concentration of African American migrants from the cotton South also began arriving in Chicago. Together, these peoples created myriad economic, cultural and geographical forces that led to changes in the city's politics, economics and industry. On any morning during this period, be it the rye of Central and Eastern Europe, the pastries of the Germans and Swedes, crusty breads of the Italians and Greeks or handmade biscuits of the cotton South, the smell of fresh-baked breads wafted through Chicago's neighborhoods. You could go to a club or bar and hear jazz to big band, blues and later rock-and-roll.

Besides the food and music, these immigrants and migrants also brought with them another aspect of old world culture—magic. It may have begun at the World's Fair in 1893, when Harry Houdini, the Yiddish-speaking son of Hungarian Jewish immigrants from Appleton, Wisconsin, had his first taste of success as a snake charmer and card sharp on the Midway. Harry Blackstone Sr., the man who many agree succeeded Houdini and Howard Thurston as the most popular magician in America, was born in Chicago in 1885. The son of German immigrants, the magician originally named Harry Bouton began performing his act, "Straight and Crooked Magic," at local vaudeville houses in 1904. Feeling the anti-Germanic sentiment after World War I, many say he changed his name to Blackstone after seeing the grandeur of Chicago's Blackstone Hotel.

Whether it was in Chicago's downtown area or the many streets, taverns and neighborhood shops, you didn't have to look hard to find card sharps, grifters, tent show evangelists, magicians, carnies, street musicians, fortune-tellers and soapbox preachers announcing the end of days. It was during this time that many of the seeds for Chicago's own Golden Age of Magic were being sown. In 1926, Laurie L. Ireland founded a magic shop. The store was later taken over by his widow, Frances Ireland, who also founded Magigals, a society of female magicians with Bess Houdini in 1938. In 1962, Ireland and her second husband, Jay Marshall, who also became dean of American Magicians, moved the store to its present location near Lincoln and Foster. Still operating as Chicago's oldest magic shop, Magic, Inc. has become one of the best-known magicians' supply houses in the nation. In its nearly one hundred years of operation, magicians including Harry Blackstone Sr. and Harry Blackstone Jr., Penn and Teller, David Copperfield and thousands of other professional and amateur magicians have spread a deck of cards or waved a magic wand purchased at Magic, Inc.

Schulien's restaurant on the North Side became an epicenter for magicians and magic fans. The tradition is said to have began when Harry Blackstone Sr. began performing tableside magic tricks in what became a hub for the German American community. Owner Matt Schulien also learned that magic could attract more customers than pickled beets, and soon he began practicing sleight of hand behind the bar. Illusionist Al Andrucci, known as "Heba Haba Al," also helped make Schulien's a nationwide destination for tourists and fellow magicians well into the 1990s.

Yet while America's Golden Age of Magic may have been between 1890 and 1930, Chicago's was just beginning. In the years following the Great Depression, everyone from movie stars to gangsters to children and adults of all ages witnessed magic in Chicago. In fact, live magic and magic acts rivaled the big bands in terms of popularity in the Windy City. Later, magicians like Marshall Brodien, with his twenty-year stint as "Wizzo the Wizard" on *Bozo's Circus* and commercials for "TV Magic Cards," continued the tradition and brought magic into the early days of live television in Chicago. Brodien's biography, *The Magical Life of Marshall Brodien*, states:

> *After World War II the Windy City had unquestionably become the magic center of the United States. The* Sphinx, *a then popular monthly magazine for magicians, had an article in the April, 1947 issue that spotlighted "The Dealers of Chicago." Listed were Jim Berg, Laurie Ireland, Sam Berland, Ed Miler and National Magic which was Jim Sherman's shop in the Palmer House. Photos of the interiors of these shops, all packed with customers, were captioned, "Chicago magic dealers are happy, well fed, and contented, with competition being the least of their worries."*

But magic was not something you just watched. Whether it was the fascinated child or the uncle or father who wanted to impress him, magic was a participatory event in which thousands of Chicagoans took part. Magicians regularly performed not only at magic shops and cabarets but also birthday parties, taverns and pool halls, as well as touring carnivals and Chicago's great amusement parks. This was especially true at Riverview, not only Chicago's legendary Mecca of rides and family fun but also home to a culture of magicians, card sharps and tricksters, circus freaks, fortune-tellers and hucksters who lurked just below the flashing lights of the Ferris wheel. Throughout the 1940s, '50s and '60s, people regularly attended magic clubs and venues and visited magic shops, especially downtown and on the North Side. Television and the rise of suburbia changed this, and by 1980, all but a few of the great magic shops and clubs were shuttered.

Now we have entered another new century, even a new millennium. Computers and the Internet have once again transformed society. Information, pictures and entire worlds can be created with a click of the mouse or the touch of a finger. Yet just as the Golden Age of Magic was born out of the changes at the turn of the last century, the popularity of magic is once again on the rise. This is especially true in Chicago. A new crop of great magicians is transforming stages, theaters, clubs, corporate venues and even homes into magical places. Almost all of them agree, and express in this book, that it has something to do with the basic need to not only satisfy a sense of childlike and romantic wonder but also a hands-on sense of human interaction. You might be able to "see" something on a computer, but you cannot feel, smell, touch and experience it in a way that live theater and live performance can. A great performance by a great magician leaves you with an experience and a true sense of amazement. This book will, like magic itself, bring back a time that once helped define the Windy City. Through vivid photos as well as the words and stories of those who experienced it, it will both reenact and preserve Chicago's great magicians, magic shops and magic clubs during a time when magicians and card sharps created Chicago's magical world of spectacle and stagecraft. But it will also bring you into a new world of romantic trickery—a world that many say may be the beginning of Chicago's second Golden Age of Magic.

CHAPTER 1

THE WORLD OF MAGIC, HOUDINI AND THE 1893 WORLD'S FAIR

It is 1893, and an eighteen-year-old from Appleton, Wisconsin, named Harry Houdini has just arrived at the Chicago World's Fair to perform at Kohl and Middleton's Dime Museum. While conjuring his many tricks and escapes, the imagination of this young magician and escape artist regularly travels outside the accepted rules and boundaries of most. Yet nothing could have prepared him for this. Looking over the Midway Pleasance, he sees over seven hundred newly built Romanesque buildings connected by a series of lagoons and canals, as if ancient Rome and Venice were both resurrected into one entity. It also features a new exhibit that combines "magic" and science, a seventy-foot tower that displays, for the first time on a large scale, the electric light. Outside the fair, the city that had largely burned to the ground during the Great Chicago Fire of 1872 was booming. Architects like Louis Sullivan and Daniel Burnham had begun to reshape the skyline of the city, as structures like the Monadnock Building redefined modern architecture.

As the young Houdini continued to gaze across the Midway, he saw not only a vast array of buildings but an even greater array of people. These included visitors from China, wearing coolie hats and embroidered silk gowns; peasants from Turkey and southeastern Europe with their colorful robes, tunics and fez-like hats; and visitors from the continents of Africa, South and Central America and southern Asia. Of course, many of the foreigners were local actors, including the young Houdini, depicting what were advertized to be exotic East Indian rituals. After all, magic is not what you see but what you perceive.

Above: Chicago's Columbian Exposition, 1893. *Courtesy Historical Findings*.

Left: Just after the Chicago World's Fair, Houdini toured as the "King of Cards" before he gained fame as an escape artist. Lithograph poster, C 1895. *McManus-Young Collection, Library of Congress*.

Dressed in a turban and white robe, Houdini would sit cross legged on a straw mat, yogi style. With his dark complexion and curly hair, few doubted the authenticity of this performer as he spread his magical tools before him. The crowd gasped as one of his talismans looked like a baby's arm that had been burned at one end. Just as the hoodoo merchants would on the South Side some fifty years later, Houdini explained that in order to create or change the path of life, you must possess the energy of it in some form. Taking a bottle of water, he would explain to the crowd, "These are the elements that will grow the mango tree."

It was the orange tree illusion, created by none other than French magician Jean Eugene Robert-Houdin, the man from whom Houdini (he added the "i") derived his stage name. As he sprinkled water on the mat, he would chant in a strange tongue. Then Houdini's brother Theo, also dressed in eastern garb, would begin playing a melody on an exotic musical instrument such as a wooden flute or lyre. Maybe he even played the "Hoochie Coochie" song. The familiar melody—to which words like, "oh the girls in France, do the hoochie-koochie dance…" would later be added—was written by fellow Chicago magician Sol Bloom for the World's Fair.

Bloom was the promoter behind "spicing up" the Midway, with displays of freaks, magicians (including hiring Houdini) and, to add a touch of sex, belly dancers. Needing an exotic, sensual-sounding song, he quickly composed the ditty. Little did he know that for the next century, the song would be performed in burlesque clubs across the world and its melody would be sung by generations of schoolboys who added lyrics like, "oh the girls in France don't wear any underpants."

As Theo continued to play his flute, Houdini would chant in a strange, nonsensical gibberish that nevertheless seemed foreign and mysterious to the crowd. Soon, both became more fervent until two small sprouts sprang from the seeds. Houdini would once again toss the shroud over the sprouts, and after sprinkling more "magic water" and "magic powder" and waving the "baby's arm," the chanting and playing would continue. After more time passed, the cloth would be removed and two small orange trees would appear. The amazed audience would shower the brothers with coins. For the first time in his life, Houdini was making a significant amount of money from his performances.

After the World's Fair, Houdini was in demand. He continued to work at Kohl and Middleton's in Chicago, working as many as twenty shows a day, mostly doing escapes. When not working, he performed card tricks in beer halls, with roaming carnivals and any other extra work he could cram in.

Then Harry and Theo received a notice to appear at Tony Pastor's Theater in New York, a vaudeville house where such stars as Irving Berlin and Al Jolson would see the spotlight. Their train fare was wired in advance—they had made the big time. Yet when they arrived, Houdini noticed his name was at the very bottom of the bill, and their big break fizzled. Houdini, who would replace Theo with his charming, petite wife, Bess, spent several months performing with the Welsh Brothers Circus, a small show without animals. Houdini performed his handcuff act alongside the "freaks" such as the fat woman and sword swallower, acts that Houdini had become familiar with while working at the World's Fair. In fact, Houdini's dexterity in removing handcuffs classified him as not a magician but a freak.

The Houdinis then toured the country as part of Dr. Hill's California Medicine Company, a traveling medicine show. Colorful as they were, these medicine shows were considered the bottom of the entertainment barrel, as hucksters in white suits and derby hats used Houdini's act to attract customers to sell phony novelties and notions, cures and elixirs for arthritis, emphysema, rheumatism and all other ailments. In the world of the supernatural, there is a fine line between magic, which presents an illusion without pretense, and elixirs, potions and powders, which claim to bring good luck and/or heal with or without results. Like many magicians, Houdini considered himself more of an artist, and he returned to the Welsh Brothers Circus. But the small circus, which may have resembled an even more primitive, leaner version of the one portrayed in the recent novel and movie *Water for Elephants*, closed for the winter. Houdini was back at square one.

Along with performing card tricks in bars, one of Houdini's side jobs was occasionally getting "arrested" and breaking out of local prisons. These events were often reported in the small-town papers, but Houdini now aimed at a big city. Like most magicians and supernatural performers, Houdini was also a superstitious man. So when he was down on his luck and needed a big break, he returned to the city where he had received his first one: Chicago.

In 1898, Chicago may have been the nation's center for corruption. Prostitutes worked unimpeded throughout the city but especially in a section just south of downtown known as the Levee, located roughly between Eleventh and Twenty-second Streets to the north and south and Clark and Dearborn to the east and west. Prostitutes of all shapes, races, sizes and ages plied their wares twenty-four hours a day, six days a week. Other forms of crime and graft, including payoffs, gang activity, phony contracts and bribery were so common that few took notice. So it was not hard for Houdini to find a policeman with plenty of spare time.

Houdini's handcuff escapes were re-created by Dennis Watkins and the House Theater. *Courtesy Dennis Watkins.*

Lieutenant Andy Rohan was the chief of detectives in the area that included the Levee. He was a large man with a walrus mustache who bore a strong resemblance to William Howard Taft. A detective and collaborator with the city's chief of police, Rohan was "generous" enough to take several hours out of his busy schedule fighting crime to be charmed by Ms. Houdini. In the meantime, Harry scoped out the locks to the cells and handcuffs. It took them two days, but Houdini was ready. After contacting several crime reporters, who also had plenty of idle time, Houdini announced that he would escape from both handcuffs and a Chicago jail. After only a minute of being incarcerated, Houdini walked into the press area waving his hands.

In a city of scams, the reporters suspected foul play. Maybe he had a hidden key. So Houdini stripped completely naked, and his short muscular frame was searched before he entered. Even his mouth was searched and somehow plastered shut. For even greater security, Rohan fastened leg irons and tightened the handcuffs. He then dangled the keys in front of Houdini's face, laughing and saying, "This is the only way you're going to get out." The policemen then put him inside a cabinet, closed the curtains and most probably smirked in confidence. After ten minutes, he walked past the reporters waving his arms. By that evening, the story had made headlines, and this new magician was now known in bars, barbershops and street corners throughout the city: Extra, Extra, Read All About It—Handcuffed Man Escapes from Chicago Jail!

Today, entertainers, studios and promoters flood all mediums with clips, videos and reviews to promote their work. But in 1898, there was no Twitter, and Houdini bought every newspaper he could, cut out the headlines and mailed them to promoters across the country. He had invented the first press kit, and his career was finally on its way—for good, with the help of the hardworking police, reporters and citizens of Chicago.

Houdini's relationship with the city continued. Chicago was one of his stops on tours that included greater escapes, séances and even making an elephant disappear. Chicago was also the location where groups of churchgoing women protested the magician and his supernatural acts, claiming that they involved the devil. But by and large, Houdini's attention then shifted to New York and later world centers of culture like London and Berlin. At the same time, however, Chicago became a major stop for the great magicians and entertainers of the day. Whether they were grand theaters or small neighborhood houses, they all worked in an era before sound film and radio in a medium known as vaudeville.

CHAPTER 2

THE EARLY STARS OF MAGIC AND CHICAGO'S VAUDEVILLE ERA

Vaudeville. For some, the name brings forth memories of the historic performers of a bygone era. For most, however, it is a distant term, faintly associated with the past and having something to do with performing.

The era began shortly after the Civil War and catered to what was an emerging middle class. Before vaudeville, entertainers performed at gatherings and inns. Vaudeville was largely performed in theaters in an environment that was alcohol free. Early vaudeville greats include Tony Pastor and Bill "Bo Jangles" Robinson. The careers of W.C. Fields, Mae West, the Marx Brothers, Bob Hope and Judy Garland began in vaudeville but reached their peak via talking pictures. Yet in a time before motion picture cameras and sound recordings that could replay and analyze every piece and act of magic, vaudeville houses became the perfect place for touring magicians. The height of vaudeville was a time when the streets and theaters were dimly lit by gas lamps, and what was then known by some as "the black art of magic" was performed partially in shadow. During this same era, magicians like Robert Herrmann, Harry Kellar and even Howard Thurston were shrouded in a haze of mystery somewhere between truth and legend. We have their black-and-white pictures and painted portraits, but we also have their grand lithograph posters. Often depicting demons, devils, witches, floating skulls and boiling cauldrons, these images fueled the imagination of a much less sophisticated public.

They performed in an era, the 1890s, that was the height of the newspaper wars between men like Joseph Pulitzer and William Randolph

Jay Marshall from upstage at the Palace Theater. *Courtesy Sandy and Susan Marshall Collection.*

Hearst. It was a time when sensationalist headlines and news editors were more than happy to forgo the facts in favor of a headline or titillating story—which played right into the hands of many touring performers. Chicago's newspapers, which numbered as many as ten and included names like the *Chicago American* and the *Chicago Evening Post*, were a major part of this trend.

Finally, although we could "see" the performers in photographs, we could not hear them or watch them move until the popularity of silent films shortly before World War I. Houdini, the name that most people still associate with magic, spent much of his career performing in vaudeville houses. Yet even before Houdini's prime and the days of Harry Blackstone Sr., magicians like Alexander Herrmann and his wife, Adelaide, Kellar, Thurston and others traveled the vaudeville circuit. As a booming metropolis and railroad hub, Chicago became a major part of what was then the most popular form of entertainment.

"I think we use the term vaudeville loosely to describe stage shows in theaters performed by troupes of basically traveling performers," says Sean Masterson, a contemporary Chicago magician whose current shows pay homage to the great performers of the past. "Thurston and Alexander Herrmann were major vaudeville stars of their time who had their own shows in grand, major theaters. At about this time, Houdini began in dime museums and smaller vaudeville houses, performing with jugglers and plate spinners."

From the 1880s until his death in 1896, Herrmann was the "King of Magic." One of sixteen children, this French-born magician was the son of Samuel Herrmann, a German doctor and magician who was said to have performed before Napoleon. His brother, Carl Herrmann, was also a famous magician who took his younger brother on tour with him throughout Europe and the United States. Soon, however, the younger Herrmann's skills became such that he became a star in his own right.

A predecessor to today's rock star, "Herrmann the Great" traveled with his own train and a luxuriously appointed private rail car that was said to have once belonged to stage actress Lilly Langtry. According to the book *Herrmann the Magician: His Life; His Secrets*, by Hardin J. Burlingame, the train made more than its share of stops in Chicago:

> As we played in Chicago more frequently than any other city, Herrmann made a point of always having something new in the way of illusions to offer…One of the most effective of these was the novelty which we called "After the Ball." In the center of the stage stood a large mirror, furnished with legs which raised off the floor so the audience could see under it and around it. Extending across the lower part was a glass shelf, which was accessible by means of steps. To the strains of Charles K. Harris' "After the Ball," I made my entrance, having apparently come from a masked ball. First I danced before a mirror; then, mounting the steps, stood on a glass

shelf. While I was thus engaged, Herrmann drew around me a three-fold screen, still leaving the mirror visible on all sides. At a shot from his pistol, the screen fell to the floor and it was seen that I had completely vanished.

Other illusions that Herrmann was said to have performed in the Windy City include "The Artist's Dream." Combining magic with theater, Herrmann depicts the scene of an artist who falls in love with a beautiful young model he has just painted. Many of the classic magic lithographs feature magicians standing next to the devil or small demons. In Herrmann's trick, Mephisto, a form of the devil, appears in a flash. Waving his hands, a beautiful young woman appears on stage and gazes lovingly at the artists. Overjoyed, the artist approaches her, but in another blaze of light, the devil waves his hand and the woman disappears.

Herrmann performed illusions at venues including at the Whitechapel Club, the Turnover Club and the Forty Club. Herrmann also performed in Chicago during the Christmas and Easter holidays. On Easter Sunday 1887, Herrmann presented every child in the audience with an Easter egg he had taken from his hat. Herrmann was also generous to Chicago's adults; when the manager of Chicago's Opera House needed $3,000, Herrmann simply wrote him a check.

When in Chicago, Herrmann regularly stayed at the Auditorium Hotel. Designed by Louis Sullivan, it is now known as the Auditorium Theater. This is where, in 1894, Herrmann celebrated his thirty-five years in show business by hosting a twenty-course dinner at the hotel, which began at midnight.

Herrmann died of heart failure in 1896 at the age of fifty-two. However, his posthumous book, *Herrmann's Book of Magic: A Black Art Exposed*, was published in Chicago in 1903 by Frederick Drake and Company.

Another great vaudeville-era magician and Herrmann's greatest rival was Harry Kellar. Born in Pennsylvania as the son of German immigrants, Kellar left home at a young age to join the Davenport Brothers Circus. He gained great fame and traveled the world, including many stops in Chicago. But while Kellar appeared at theaters and events in Chicago, such as the McVickers Theater, there is no record of any unusual happenings or notable links with the Windy City.

The man who many believe to be Kellar's magical successor, Howard Thurston, however, had a direct and lasting link to Chicago. Like Kellar, Thurston ran away to join the circus before he hit his teens. Thurston, like Houdini, performed at the 1893 Columbian Exposition at Chicago.

While Houdini's dark complexion and curly hair enabled him to gain employment as an east Indian flute player at the Tunisian Village, Thurston

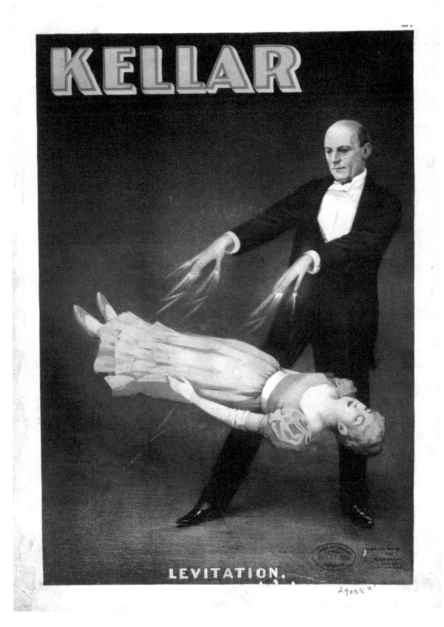

Harry Kellar was the first American-born magician to become a "superstar" of vaudeville. Poster by Stonebridge Lithograph Co., 1894. *Courtesy Library of Congress.*

was able to earn wages as a "barker" at the African Dahomey Village on the Midway Plaisance at the western edge of the fairgrounds. While Houdini's act did involve some magic, Thurston's employment did not require any sleight of hand. Instead, it used sleight of clothing. Standing in front of the village, which was the brainchild of Frenchman Xavier Penne, Thurston shouted to waiting passersby a speech that resembled the following: "Direct from Africa, see the African culture, the savage, untamed, wild natives, performing exotic dances, that few have laid eyes upon…"

Yet it wasn't Thurston's speech that drew in the curious crowds. Photos from the exhibit strongly suggest that the "wild natives performing exotic dances" were nearly topless native women. Just as many teens from a bygone era gawked at photos of tribal females in *National Geographic*, the fact that the females were "savages" allowed for a loophole in what was generally considered the mores of the time. The same was true of another performer. Performing at the base of the George Ferris's magnificent wheel was a Syrian dancer named Farida Mazar Spyropoulous, also known as Fatima. Dancing what is now known as a "belly dance" in an area called "Little Egypt," the voluptuous young dancer allowed her body to undulate back and forth and up and down. In the process, she exposed skin in places that would not be accepted by a "non-savage."

This act was witnessed not only by Thurston but also his younger brother Harry. According to the book *The Last Greatest Magician in the World* by Jim Steinmeyer, the Thurston brothers prowled the Midway looking for ideas. Yet while Howard found his inspiration in magic and a career that would, in sheer magic and card play, rival that of Houdini, Harry Thurston found a less taxing, more lucrative business.

Harry made friends with many of the hootchie-kootchie dancers and exhibitors on the Midway. Deciding to stay in Chicago, he became a grifter and con artist, ingratiating himself with many of the politicians in the city's corrupt First Ward. Known as the Levee District, it was the home of gamblers, drunks, gangsters and a prostitute district larger than those of New York and even New Orleans. The younger Thurston also made friends with the ward's politicians, including First Ward Alderman Michael "Hinky Dink" Kenna. Standing all of five foot one, he was perhaps the most corrupt politician in the annals of Chicago history—a tall feat indeed.

With Kenna's help, Harry Thurston established a dime museum on South State Street. Basically a stationary carnival freak show, it contained photos and live performances from deformed twins, fire eaters and even the unborn fetuses of Siamese twins soaked in formaldehyde. But nestled in the back room was the biggest attraction, the "Maid of Mystery." A forerunner to the "peep show," it featured burlesque performers who removed everything but their shoes. After bribing Kenna and the local police, there was still plenty of money left over. This money was used to help jumpstart Thurston's brother's career. For many years, Harry's money helped even the balance sheet for Howard's vaudeville show, which, like Herrmann's and Kellar's, featured railroad cars carrying expensive equipment, signs and assistants. It is said that when he was not touring, Howard Thurston took advantage of Chicago's position of a rail hub and his younger brother's spacious building to store his magic equipment on the second floor of the museum.

Yet as Howard became more successful, he became less reliant on his brother's financial assistance. After World War I, when the name Thurston rivaled that of any vaudeville performer in the nation, he was able to pay his brother's loans back. At about that time, Chicago's Levee District was finally beginning to break up, as the houses of ill repute became less ostentatious and Chicago's downtown began its long journey toward family decency. The younger Thurston now needed his brother. Changing the dime museum's name to Thurston's World Museum, he advertized the fact that he was the brother of the famous magician. At this time, Thurston made a decision that had a profound effect on magic. At events like the World's Fair and with some traveling carnivals, magic and magicians like Thurston and Houdini were still occasionally linked to some of the seedier elements of the entertainment world. But thanks to the financial rewards of vaudeville houses across the national circuit, magicians were able to gain greater income and, for the most part, break away from the circuses and carnivals. With his position as a vaudeville star, the elder Thurston decided that his magic was a show not only for curious adults but their children and families as well. He strongly protested his brother's naming the museum Thurston's and having any association between hootchie-kootchie dancers and magic. It seems that Howard's morality won out, as Harry sent back a letter stating, "Will say I closed the Thurston Museum a week ago and have got my old place back, The Royal. I will now call it Wonderland Museum. If I open another place again I will never mention the word magic in any way. I am doing fine and not running any hootch dancers at all."

Another man who had a hand in Thurston's success was a magician named Okito. Born in the Netherlands as Tobias "Theodore" Bamberg, Okito was the sixth generation of magicians known as the Bamberg Magical Dynasty. A childhood accident left him nearly deaf, and Bamberg performed his magic almost entirely in pantomime. He also donned dark makeup, a

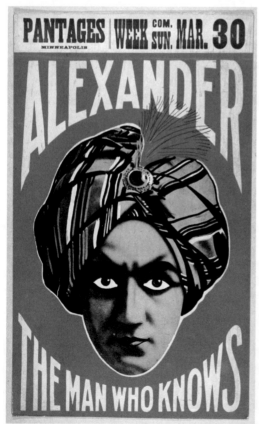

Above: Theodore Bamberg, "Okito," began his American career in vaudeville. *Photo by author.*

Left: Alexander, one of the many colorful but lesser-known vaudeville magicians. *McManus-Young Collection, Library of Congress.*

coolie hat and long silk robes. In 1907, Bamberg moved to the United States, where he worked building sets and magical props for Thurston. Bamberg then opened a magic shop, Bamberg Magic and Novelty Co., in New York, which thrived for many years. After touring South America, he moved back to his native country. As a Jew, he began to see storm clouds on the horizon and moved back to the United States shortly before World War II. Once in the United States, he settled in Chicago. For many years, he worked at Chicago's downtown magic stores and became great friends with many magicians, including Jay Marshall. Okito died in 1963 and is buried in Westlawn Cemetery in Norridge, Illinois.

Not all vaudeville magicians, however, were as successful as Kellar, Thurston or Houdini. In fact, these pre–electronic age "superstars" were the exception to the rule in the world of vaudeville. Masterson says:

> *Vaudeville magicians and other performers had a very tough go of it. They went from show to show on rail cars, and they would usually have to get off the train at some kind of crossroads in the middle of nowhere. It was often hot or cold, and they had to sit in the dark lugging equipment, surrounded by other performers or drunken musicians waiting for a change that sometimes took hours to arrive. Unlike other performers who sometimes travel in troupes, magicians who were vaudeville headliners had to arrange the whole show. That included trying to get in touch with an advance man, if there was one, in the days before telephones. There usually wasn't, so it was their job to help distribute posters, sell tickets and do just about everything you can imagine to make the show go on.*

At first, this was the case for Houdini. After the World's Fair in 1893, he paid his bills by becoming a regular performer at one of Chicago's first acknowledged vaudeville houses. Opened in 1892 by C.E. Kohl and George Middleton, the establishment was known as Kohl and Middleton's Dime Museum or the West Side Museum. Although there were three locations, Houdini is said to have performed at 150 North Clark Street, as well as 300 South State Street. It was in Chicago that Houdini received the call to travel as part of the Orpheum Circuit, a series of nationwide vaudeville houses. As time when on, he would appear in London and Berlin and tour the world. Yet even though Houdini eventually appeared in many popular silent films, he also worked his way up to being the highest-paid and most popular vaudeville performer in the country. In 1926, he opened a one-man show on Broadway, *Houdini*. Performing to record crowds and rave reviews, he then took the show on the road. His last performance in Chicago was at the Princess Theater in April 1926. Houdini was on the vaudeville circuit in Montreal when he voluntarily took the blows to his stomach that would eventually claim his life on October 31, 1926. This marked the end of an era in two ways—the death of one of vaudeville's greatest draws and, in 1927, the creation of the sound film. "Many scholars think that true vaudeville ended in 1927, with the advent of sound in the movies," Masterson says.

A short time later, the theaters that formerly composed the Orpheum Circuit were taken over by RKO Studios. Although some artists like Charlie Chaplin and Gloria Swanson never enjoyed the same success as they had in silent films, the verbal repartee of vaudeville greats like Fields, West, the Marx Brothers and Bob Hope easily made the transition from vaudeville to talking pictures.

Some magicians continued to perform in Chicago movie theaters before or between films as part of "stage shows," but the Great Depression put a damper on these more lavish events. Although Thurston still performed, the deaths of Houdini and Kellar signaled a profound shift in the world of magic. In order to cut expenses, most magicians stopped or cut back on their touring. The end of vaudeville also meant that most of the theaters were no longer available as outlets for magicians to perform. This resulted in the scaling down of lavish sets, paid assistants and train cars full of props and even animals.

Yet just as fast as you could say "abracadabra," magic shed its old skin and gained a new life. More and more, the art was performed in smaller nightclubs, bars and restaurants. Some say that it was perfected in Chicago's famous Schulien's restaurant. Wherever the truth lies, it is certain that Chicago magicians, Chicago clubs and Chicago audiences helped to lead the evolution of the form into what is now known as "close-up magic." Furthermore, while Los Angles had its Hollywood stars and New York had Broadway, magicians were allowed to step into the forefront of entertainment in Chicagoland. This, along with the postwar economic boom, led to what many call the "Golden Age of Magic" in Chicago. Before that transformation began, Houdini had one more great accomplishment before his death. It was an act performed worldwide, but its beginnings, and its climax, occurred in Chicago.

CHAPTER 3

HOUDINI, CHICAGO AND THE GREAT DEBUNKING OF SPIRITUALISM

The setting is a large, Queen Anne–style house with a white picket fence, wraparound railing, tended gardens and wicker rocking chair on the porch. Inside, past the glass chandelier and oak staircase, a woman in a gray dress is seated at a long wooden table in a darkened room. She is surrounded by people, all holding hands, staring at the woman intently. The woman begins talking.

"I can see now. We have crossed to the other side. My signal is coming in. There is a light. The smell, it smells like lilacs and magnolias. It is beautiful on the other side. Soft colors pervade like the end of a rainbow…I can hear music playing."

As she speaks, the people around the table crowd closer. "Does anybody here know a man named Carl?"

An elderly woman clutches her breastbone. "Carl…that was my husband."

Lights flash. Curtains ruffle. A low, croaking voice is heard in the distance. "Emma…is that you?

The elderly woman, dressed in a gown with pearls and all the finery of an early twentieth-century aristocrat, cries out, "Carl, it's me…I can hear you!"

The woman at the table begins shaking. A trumpet suddenly appears, floating in the sky above the chandelier, playing mysterious notes. Tambourines rattle and float through the sky. The woman at the table begins shaking as if in a trance.

The lights go dim, on, off, on, off. The people around the table begin clamoring. "I can see Carl now. He has gray hair and is wearing a dark suit."

"Yes!" the aristocratic woman shouts. "He had gray hair, and he wore dark suits. That is Carl, my husband. What is he saying? What is he trying to tell us?"

This was the approximate scene at hundreds of events in the late nineteenth and early twentieth centuries. Sometimes they were called séances. Other times they were advertised as meetings with clairvoyants, spiritualists or sessions at an Ouija board. Whatever the label, they were the rage of their era, as people from poor parishioners to Mary Todd Lincoln, Sir Arthur Conan Doyle and wealthy industrialists and merchants all clamored to communicate with the dead.

The connection between spiritualism and magic in the United States can be traced back to Harry Kellar joining the Davenport Brothers and Fay's in 1869. Kellar would eventually compete with Alexander Herrmann as the "World's Greatest Magician" and was later lionized by Houdini. His last magical act was before the Society of American Magicians, where he was carried off in triumph by his fellow illusionists. Yet even though they first billed themselves as magicians, the group, which consisted of Ira Erastus Davenport, William Henry Davenport, William Fay and later Kellar, gained fame as being among the early practitioners of the Spiritual movement in the United States.

Physically, the four men could well have been the model for the cover of Smith Brothers Cough Drops. Their greatest attraction was the "Sprit Box" illusion. Audiences would watch as the brothers were tied up and then entered a closed box filled with musical instruments. Once inside, the instruments would begin playing. Since the brothers could not move, they claimed that it was spirits that made the instruments sound. A hit with an unsophisticated, uneducated public, Kellar toured with the Davenport Brothers until 1873. At that time, Kellar and Fay embarked on a tour of Mexico and South America. Although some magic was performed, much of their shows consisted of demonstrations of Spiritualism, the supernatural and communicating with the dead. While in Brazil, they appeared before Emperor Dom Pedro III, and records estimate that they were able to make as much as $10,000 a day, which is almost $203,000 adjusted to inflation.

There were profits to be made in Spiritualism. In a city where crime, the dodge and making a fast buck was a way of life, this news did not go unnoticed in Chicago. In fact, it was about the same time, the early 1870s, when Chicago's most infamous Spiritualists, the Bangs Sisters, began to make their mark on the Windy City. Although Elizabeth was born in Kansas in 1860, Mary Bangs was born in Chicago in 1864. The daughters of a medium, the entire Bangs family began performing regular séances. These acts were performed at their home, which, according to the Map of Chicago Magic, was located at 3 South Elizabeth Street just west of Chicago's downtown region.

An article in the *Religio-Philosophical Journal* stated that people would file into the Bangses' home to witness messages from the dead appearing on slates, furniture flying about the room, a shaved cat that was said to be a spirit and their modified version of the Davenport Brothers' musical cabinet.

On April 17, 1888, the *Washington Post* reported that the "Notorious Bangs Sisters" were responsible for a series of fraudulent acts against numerous wealthy clients. One, photographer Henry Jestram, was fleeced out of vast amounts of money and ended up dying in an insane asylum. Although they were arrested numerous times by Chicago police, the Bangs Sisters stayed one step ahead of the law by introducing new elements to their act, including such novel items as painted portraits, letters and other writings from the dead. They became most famous for their portraits. Seemingly appearing from out of nowhere and developed before the client's eyes, experts have surmised that sketches were made beforehand, hidden and slowly moved forward into the light by a free hand while the subjects were not looking.

The Bangs Sisters convinced Dr. Isaac Funk, of *Funk and Wagnall's Encyclopedia* fame, to pay $1,500 for ghost portraits. Mary Bangs convinced chemical titan Henry H. Graham to marry her after a séance in which she told the wealthy industrialist that his dead wife had given her a signal from the grave that it was okay for them to marry. Other victims included one of the main investors in the first typewriter, G.W.N. Yost, who parted with much of his fortune after seeing the "spirit typewriter" type him a message. All in all, the Bangs Sisters went through five husbands and numerous wealthy millionaires and industrialists and took the paychecks and savings of even more poor working Chicagoans.

Although the Bangs Sisters were the most notorious, the streets and alleys of Chicago were filled with hundreds of Spiritualists who were more than eager to perform séances for a price. The same was true throughout the United States and even the world.

Houdini was first exposed to Spiritualism while working at Chicago's World's Fair. Legend has it that a man known as Zan Zac, a former magician who Houdini had seen, hung out his shingle as a séance specialist. The con artist apparently sold a man with degenerating vision a bucket of "special spirit mud." A short time later, he regained his eyesight. The same gentleman, now assured of Zan Zac's powers, was ready to pay any price, for he was sure that Zan Zac could bring his long-dead wife back to life—at least for a short time. Zan Zac was more than ready to oblige and quickly found a young woman who fit the description that the gentleman had given him. With all of his experience as a magician making people disappear, Zan Zac saw no problem performing this "appearing" act.

Lights were turned off. Zan Zac and the elderly Chicagoan began a séance. Upon seeing the "vision" of his wife, the old codger got up and kissed her. Apparently, his eyesight was not completely healed, as the man was sure that this was her. As the man wanted to spend time with his bride, Zan Zac convinced the young woman to continue the con. They met at a bridal suite, but upon seeing the beautiful young woman, the old man perished from a heart attack. Zan Zac left him on Chicago's cold streets. Houdini winced at what he saw as unscrupulous practices to say the least. But as a young magician who could barely pay for a room himself, he was in no position to express his displeasure.

Most people who are familiar with Houdini know that he adored his mother with a sense of devotion that bordered on mania. He sent her letters almost every day, often containing large sums of money. One time, he bought her a jeweled dress sewn for the queen of England. Friends wondered how his devoted wife, Bess, could survive such a relationship. When his mother died, Houdini was despondent. Although he had sworn off Spiritualism, many of his friends, including Kellar and author Arthur Conan Doyle, had a background in it. Desperate, the Great Houdini went to séance after séance hoping to hear his mother's voice. What this veteran illusionist saw instead was seedy, shabby trickery performed by unskilled scoundrels. His displeasure turned to anger, which then manifested into fury.

Slowly, Houdini began to mount a campaign against the Spiritualists. He sent a team of magicians and scientists to séances, where they found the dead were brought back via tricks of light, double exposed photographs, hidden wires, speakers and filters. Signals to helpers concealed behind curtains or in darkened corridors were given via hand signs, hidden buzzers and levers that were placed under the séance tables.

Houdini began to tour the country again, but this time he wasn't performing magic per se but using his magical skills to demonstrate how Spiritualists were scamming the public. He lectured at colleges, universities and vaudeville theaters and on the radio to denounce the practice. On February 26, 1926, Houdini testified before a U.S. Congressional Committee in support of House Bill 8989, which would ban Spiritualism in the District of Columbia. He testified again in May of that year, visually showing how he could "play" a trumpet that floated in the air and write words on a blank slate. Despite his testimony, the bill failed.

It was in Chicago that Houdini experienced his climactic public relations and later legal battle against the séance scam artists. It began when Houdini commenced an eight-week run at Chicago's Princess Theater, located on Clark Street just south of Jackson Boulevard. Night after night he showed crowds, often composed of children and the poor, whom he allowed to attend for free, the various forms of chicanery involved in Spiritualism. At the same time, Houdini had a team of magicians, photographers and scientists, paid at his expense, scouring the city to turn up fraudulent mediums.

The book *Houdini, the Untold Story* reports how a team of Houdini's men attended a séance by Ms. Minnie Reichart. It was held in a house on South Emerald Avenue, a street that begins just south of the Chicago Loop and ends at the beginning of what was then the Chicago Stockyards. The night began with over twenty people sitting at a table holding hands. Songs like "Nearer to God Than Thee" and "Yes Sir, That's My Baby" played throughout the room. The crowd was sitting while an illusion of Chief Blackhawk was speaking through a trumpet in guttural tones when flash bulbs exploded across the room. Reporters from the *Chicago American* began taking pictures behind curtains. More pictures were taken, and the reporters rushed out of the room. The medium's sister followed them out to the lawn, where she attacked the photographers. Men were slapped and scratched. Flash guns were smashed, and hats were crushed into the green grass. But the camera and film survived, and the pictures developed without incident. The next morning, an incriminating picture adorned the front page of the *Chicago American*.

That morning, Houdini replied, "This picture is worth thousands of hats because it shows up one of the frauds who have been taking money from Chicagoans by pretending to be spirits."

Houdini continued to perform his show at the Princess, and after the show, he handed out lists that contained the names and addresses of fraudulent mediums. Seeing this, the medium Herbert Breedlove, who ran a séance parlor on South Dearborn Street, filed charges of libel and harassment against Houdini in Cook County court. The trial was held on South Clark Street before Judge Francis Borelli. Out of curiosity, the judge asked Breedlove if he could summon the spirits in the courtroom. The medium claimed that he didn't have the right environment. Houdini then offered Breedlove, or anyone, $1,000 if he could conjure the nickname his father had given him. Breedlove declined the offer, and the charges were later dropped.

Houdini held free shows at Chicago's Prince Theater in order to debunk séances. *Courtesy Darby and Melissa Culler.*

Then, as if conjured by a magic wand, an elderly couple arrived unexpectedly in Houdini's dressing room. Mrs. Ernest Bennington was a former Spiritualist who was responsible for training and mentoring some of the city's most notorious séance artists out of her North Side apartment. She was also ordained by the National Spiritualists Association.

Houdini introduced Ms. Bennington at a press conference at the Sherman Hotel. But instead of speaking to reporters, Bennington began a séance. Lights darkened. Trumpets floated in the air, voices hummed in low tones and hands floated in the air. Then Ms. Bennington began to reveal her secrets. The trumpet sounds were made by attaching two trumpets together. Breathing into one, the sounds came out the other. She then showed her ventriloquist skills, "throwing" different voices throughout the room. Just as Alexander Herrmann had done, she had painted a glove with luminous paint and then put it in front of a black velvet background. Other diversions were placed under her skirt, and signals were given while she fiddled with her hair. The press duly recorded everything in both print and photos, and once again, the newspaper headlines carried the day for Houdini's cause both in Chicago and across the nation.

Houdini had finally turned the tide. Although there would always be a segment of the population who believed in psychics, the average American was at least aware of their dangers, and many were kept from their clutches. Yet the belief in Spiritualism and the raising of the dead did not go away, even in the Houdini family. In 1936, ten years after his death, Bess Houdini held a séance on Halloween, Houdini's birthday, in the hope that she could hear the voice of her husband from the other side.

On Halloween night 1961, a young Sandy Marshall and his father, Jay Marshall, the owner of Magic, Inc., gathered with several other magicians to try to resurrect the spirit of Houdini. The séance, which was heavily attended by members of the Chicago press, was held at Jay Marshall's home at 804 South Wesley in Oak Park. While sitting around a long table, the men set a skull on a Ouija board. A drum, an arrow and busts of Houdini and Bess also adorned the scene. Apparently, they were trying to take Houdini up on his offer of $10,000 to any Spiritualist who could accomplish his feats. Previous séances had been held at midnight on October 30. Thinking that all others had made a minor mistake, this one was held at midnight on October 31. First, the men stared at a glass of water, hoping that the liquid, which is known to transport spirits, would do so. After no results, the seven men held hands and grasped the Ouija board. Fingers turned white, but the skull was unmoved. In an effort to communicate by sound, the sitters held up the small drum, hoping Houdini would make his spirit heard through music. Finally, the men stared at the skull, hoping the jaws would move.

"Lo and behold," Sandy Marshall said some fifty years later, "Houdini did not show up. But it did make front-page news. On November 1, 1961, the headline on the *Chicago Sun-Times* read 'Houdini No Broom Rider.' A lot of press guys were there, and between the jokes and the Scotch, they had a great time. Also," Marshall continued, "a magician named Don Allen was opening a show at the Magic Ranch, so it turned out to be a great publicity stunt, so it worked quite well."

Yet even though Houdini's ghost has yet to appear, séances and the hope of seeing the great Houdini still haunt Chicago's magic scene. Beginning on Halloween night 2001, necromancer Neil Tobin and the Chicago Chapter of the Society of American Magicians have held an annual séance at the city's Excalibur (now Castle Chicago) nightclub. Located at Dearborn and Ontario in the heart of the city's River North District, the club is a giant limestone building dating back to just after the Great Chicago Fire. It is said to that employees have sworn that they have seen apparitions in the building since it opened as a nightclub. Perhaps one of the few buildings in Chicago that could double as a castle, it is the perfect place to re-create a Victorian-era séance.

CHAPTER 4

HARRY BLACKSTONE SR.

CHICAGO NATIVE AND THE
LAST "KING OF MAGIC"

To many in the 1930s, '40s and '50s, the name Blackstone was the most famous in all of magic. Before that, he was considered to be a competitor of Houdini, and his innovations are still used by many magicians today. During a sixty-year career that spanned vaudeville, nightclubs, radio, the Golden Age of Magic and into the television age, Harry Blackstone Sr. even starred in his own radio show and had a comic book series based on him.

"Blackstone was the last of the four greats: Keller, Thurston, Houdini and, of course, Blackstone, whose professional career began in 1910 and lasted until 1955," Jeff Taylor, director of the American Museum of Magic in Marshall, Michigan, says. "While Houdini was known for his escapes, Blackstone became known for his elegant stage shows, which often lasted two and a half hours and had tons of equipment and dozens of people; it was a real theatrical show."

Harry Bouton was born as the son of German immigrants in Chicago in 1885. In 1893, at about the same time Houdini and Thurston were performing at the World's Fair, Bouton received his first magic trick as a present for his birthday. At the age of twelve, he saw Keller perform at the second incarnation of the McVickers Theater, designed by Adler and Sullivan and located near Madison and Wabash. As a teenager, he followed in his father's footsteps, working as a carpenter and cabinetmaker in homes on Chicago's North Side. He first began performing professionally under the name Frederick.

"A magician named Frederick had banners and posters printed up with his name, but he went bankrupt," Taylor says of a practice commonly done by performers in the days before mass communication. "So he [Blackstone] figured he might as well take them and change his name."

With the coming of World War I, however, came an anti-Germanic backlash, as things like sauerkraut became taboo in many households. Being named after a prominent German/Prussian king fell into that category, and in 1917, he changed his name to Blackstone, which many scholars say was taken after visiting Chicago's wondrous Blackstone Hotel.

Seeing the success of Houdini, Blackstone's first big vaudeville acts contained many escapes and acts of underwater daring. In fact, Houdini saw Blackstone as a rival and copycat.

"Blackstone did escapes, including the 'underwater crate,' which was his answer to Houdini's milk can escape," Taylor says. As Taylor speaks, he is surrounded not only by colorful show posters of Blackstone, Houdini and hundreds of other magicians but also by many of the personal effects of the great magicians that can be seen at the museum, including a large black iron container used by Blackstone himself early in his career "Houdini saw this and did whatever he could to keep him out of the Society of American Magicians (SAM), as he didn't like other escape artists. But while Houdini was short and very muscular, Blackstone was a tall, lanky guy, which made it not only more difficult to perform escapes out of small areas but, with his long legs and skinny arms, made him not look as much of an athlete."

It could be said that when he was clad in black tank swimsuits, Blackstone's long limbs combined with what was to become his trademark shock of wild, curly hair made him look somewhat like an ostrich. Yet when dressed in the long black "tails" of the era, his long frame made him quite the dashing figure. So it was on the vaudeville stage that Blackstone began to make his mark. Part of it was his magnificent charm and stage personality, but much of it came from the many innovations that he added to the catalogue of magic.

Some of his more notable tricks include the vanishing horse and the dancing handkerchief, but he is most admired and copied by magicians for his floating light bulb illusion. "Blackstone held it in his hands, and it lit with no chord," Taylor says about the bulb, which is said to have been made by Thomas Edison. "He then floated the bulb into the air, where once again, it lit. Finally, it moved out over the top of the audience, still floating through the air, still lit."

The bulb, which now sits in the Smithsonian Institution, is an image often used along with items like the top hat, wand, doves and locks and chains as a visual symbol of magic itself. Visually, however, the bulb was not the only amazing thing presented at Blackstone's shows. Competing on the vaudeville and, later, Broadway and Las Vegas stages with the likes of Ziegfeld and the Rockettes, Blackstone surrounded himself with not one but a bevy of beautiful women. He also added to a common and now standard part of many stage magic shows: the elements of suspense and danger. This was done primarily through his interpretation of the old "sawing the lady in half" trick.

"While many magicians of the era sawed a lady inside of a box, where things could perhaps be hidden, dropped or maneuvered, Blackstone took the lady out of the box," Taylor says. "And while they used a handsaw, which some think could also be manipulated, Blackstone used an [electric] buzz saw, which was not only faster, more dangerous and unpredictable, but it made that high-pitched, buzzing noise, which only added to the overall drama on stage."

As Taylor continues to talk, he walks over to a series of crates that take up much of the space in the back end of the museum. They are old black trunks with heavy wooden doors and pounded tin ornamentation, exactly like the ones commonly associated by vaudeville performers or the trunks that were loaded onto steamships. Taylor opens a vertical trunk, a magician's tool kit, which holds dozens of pop-out drawers housing various props like rings and ropes, as well as saws and other tools used by Blackstone (the son of a cabinetmaker) and his staff to craft their stage magic. Yet the trunks are not the traditional flat black of the vaudeville era. Instead, the are painted orange, which gives us a glimpse into the mind of a man who was not only an innovative and creative force but also, like many magicians, a man of great logic.

"Blackstone mounted very large, complicated shows, which traveled the country by train," Taylor says. "They were constantly in and out of train stations, setting up in theaters, then leaving and moving on. In order to save time and confusion, he painted all of his trunks bright orange, and it became known in show business that if it was an orange trunk, it was Blackstone's. So much so that it is said that his staff always had a can of orange paint on hand, and if they saw something they liked, it suddenly became orange."

The American Museum of Magic is located in Marshall, Michigan, just east of Kalamazoo. It is a short drive from Colon, Michigan. After being born and raised in Chicago, growing up in the hustle and bustle of the city's theaters, streetcars and magnificent downtown, Blackstone decided to move to Colon, a town 150 miles northeast of Chicago, as he approached middle

Harry Blackstone Sr. is buried with his son and grandson in Colon, Michigan. *Photo by author.*

age. "He grew up in the city and largely performed in large towns, so it seems he needed someplace quiet to go when he was not working," Taylor says.

Driving toward Colon on a hot summer afternoon, it is indeed peaceful. Surrounded by farms and a few scarce homesteads, the rare car and truck is often accompanied by an Amish horse and buggy or a young Amish man making his way on a bicycle. A sign above the town reads "Magic Capital of the World." It gained its title primarily because it was the home of Blackstone and his partner, Percy Abbott. The two formed a large magic supply company there in 1934. Being the more famous of the two, Blackstone left to earn his way on the Depression-era roads, leaving Abbott to mind the store. Legend has it that Blackstone returned to find what he saw as "irregularities" in the books. A feud erupted, and Abbott bought out Blackstone's interest. Today, Abbott's Magic Company is another of America's great magic stores.

But Blackstone had bigger fish to fry. In 1941, the comic book *Blackstone the Magic Detective* hit drugstores throughout America. In 1948, the comic was turned into a radio program beamed throughout the nation. Blackstone also toured tirelessly for the USO and other organizations, entertaining and supporting the troops during World War II. As the television age approached, Blackstone became one of the biggest names, making regular appearances on *The Tonight Show* with Steve Allen and many others.

Blackstone also made regular stops in Chicago. Matt Schulien, who went on to convert Chicago's Schulien's restaurant into one of the greatest magical spaces in the country, decided that he wanted to became a magician after seeing Blackstone perform after a show in the Chicago restaurant. As a young man, future owner of Magic, Inc. Jay Marshall also saw Blackstone perform. Not only did Blackstone sign his autograph, but he also walked with Marshall to a liquor store, where he bought a pint of White Horse Scotch. The great magician not only wished the young novice luck in his career but also expressed the deep desire that they would remain in contact as friends, which they did.

In 1955, Blackstone retired. In doing so, he passed not only his name but his entire act to his son, Harry Blackstone Jr. A great magician in his own right, Blackstone Jr. became known to children throughout America in the 1960s for his television commercials for PF Flyers and his PF Magic Wedge Kit, which was used to sell the popular brand of sneaker. Blackstone Jr. also appeared on TV shows like *The Tonight Show* but aimed much of his "magic" to children, which included working for D.C. Comics and appearing on the *Super Mario Brothers* cartoon and PBS's *Square One*, where he used magic to teach mathematics.

Today, Harry Blackstone Sr., his son, Harry Blackstone Jr., and grandson Harry Blackstone III, who died tragically at the age of twenty-four, are all buried under a single monument in Colon, Michigan. A large cement sphere vaguely resembling a flame, it sits in a small country graveyard in the heart of the Midwest, along with the markers of the townspeople of Colon, some going back to the Civil War. Blackstone's grave is also surrounded by the remains of many other magicians who chose to be buried near the great Blackstone.

"Harry Blackstone Sr. was in Chicago during the World's Fair, saw greats like Keller perform there and then he himself became a part of the era of the great touring shows," Taylor says. "He was born before silent film and records but lived through many eras, including vaudeville, radio, silent film, film and into the modern age of television."

CHAPTER 5

MAGIC, INC.

THE SOUL OF CHICAGO MAGIC

The heart of Chicago magic lies deep inside its many performers, but if Chicago magic had a soul, it would be located inside Magic, Inc. Established in 1926, it is the oldest magic shop in Chicago and one of the oldest businesses in the city. Its customers have included David Copperfield, Penn and Teller, Doug Henning, Harry Blackstone Sr., Harry Blackstone Jr. and almost every man, woman and child who has donned a top hat, waved a wand or made a card disappear in Chicagoland. Yet the list of accolades is just beginning. Its longtime owners have included magician Laurie Ireland and his wife, Frances Ireland. A great magician in her own right, Mrs. Ireland authored more than ten books on magic and broke cultural barriers when she began the organization Magigals with Bess Houdini in 1936. After L. Ireland's death, Ireland's Magic was transformed into Magic, Inc. It was co-owned by Jay Marshall, Frances's second husband and one of the most noted American magicians of the twentieth century. Named dean of the Society of American Magicians, Marshall appeared on the *Ed Sullivan Show* fourteen times and has shared the stage or studio with Frank Sinatra, Paul Robeson, Liberace and Walter Cronkite, to name just a few.

In 2005, Magic, Inc. was passed on to Alexander "Sandy" Marshall, Jay Marshall's eldest son and grandson of Al Baker, the dean of the Society of American Magicians from 1941 to 1951. A prominent magician in his own right, Marshall is also a two-time Emmy-winning television writer, filmmaker and playwright who splits his time between the bright lights of Broadway and the waving wands of Magic, Inc. Marshall is also the author of the book

Magic, Inc. as it stands today. *Photo by author.*

Beating a Dead Horse, a memoir of Jay and Sandy Marshall's lives in magic. Sitting underneath the stage of Magic, Inc.'s performance and lecture area, Marshall begins to talk about the store's renowned past.

"Magic, Inc. began as Ireland's Magic by magician Laurie Ireland at his home in Oak Park 1926," Marshall says. "After he married my stepmother, the shop moved to 109 North Dearborn, but Ireland drank himself to death, so the shop was taken over by his wife, Frances."

As he stands beneath such magical lore as posters of Harry Houdini and his magical "idol," early French magician Robert Houdin, and an old storefront sign for TV Magic Cards, Marshall begins to explain his father's involvement in the store.

"My father and Ms. Ireland met at a magic convention in the late 1930s," Marshall says. "Jay was a young man, but the magic world could tell there was something between them. They continued a long-distance relationship via letters, but after Laurie died, things happened rapidly, and they were married in 1954."

After their marriage, Marshall assumed co-ownership of the shop. Marshall, however, was continually traveling around the nation and the world, performing in London, Paris, Tokyo, Sidney and all parts in between. Once he moved to Chicago, his presence was also omniscient. His accomplishments and whereabouts could fill a six-hundred-page book (see

Beating a Dead Horse), but a short list of some of Marshall's major Chicago appearances include *Bozo's Circus* and early Chicago television productions such as *Kup's Show*, *The Crome Circle*, *T-- Magic and You*, *The Magic Ranch*, *It's Magic*, *Sunday in Chicago* and countless local newscasts.

"My father was the go-to magician on *Bozo's Circus* after Marshall Brodien," Marshall says. "He played the Palmer House, Chicago Theater— he was everywhere."

So busy that even though he owned half of Magic, Inc., he generally left things up to his wife. "Frances ran the day-to-day operations of the store and ran it with an iron fist," Marshall says.

She ran it so well that, despite Marshall's continuous touring schedule, the couple decided they needed to expand. Pooling together their limited resources, they purchased a building at 5082 North Lincoln Avenue. Although they did keep the downtown location open for a short duration with magician Lee Wayne behind the counter, it was obvious that Chicago's Loop was already feeling the negative effects of the great move to the suburbs. The new shop had plenty of parking for the new automobile era. It was also close to neighborhoods on the north and northern suburbs, making it more family friendly. But the biggest advantage was space. The building was over twenty thousand square feet and had space for a warehouse, a print shop for the many publications Magic, Inc. put out, offices and a backroom theater. Later on, they bought the property next door, which formerly housed stables for the Chicago Police Department and later became a speakeasy owned by Al Capone.

The new space also had a second floor. With Jay Marshall's outgoing, social nature and connection to artists and magicians throughout the world, many found a temporary or even a semi-permanent home above Magic, Inc.

"A few of the better-known magicians who stayed upstairs included Harry Blackstone Jr., Patrick Page and Bill Mc Comb," Marshall says. "But just about any traveling magician coming by had a home at Magic, Inc., as sometimes during conventions we had as many as twenty people staying up there. My father even put a nameplate on the two apartments; one was the Don Lawton Suite and the other was the Charlie Miller Suite."

Johnny Thompson, a Chicago-born magician who got his start at Riverview but eventually became a regular at the Playboy Club and the Magic Castle in Los Angeles, was another frequent guest.

"Magic, Inc. was my second home," Thompson said in *Beating a Dead Horse*. "I was there probably more than in my own apartment. When I was doing trade shows I would practically live there. Jay would come down for coffee and just be there to help. That was my hangout from 1963 until 1974. Sometimes I'd even go behind the counter and sell for Jay, just for kicks."

Magic, Inc.'s official grand opening coincided with a ten-day magic celebration from January 2 to 11, 1964. Magicians throughout the country showed up for the event, including Don Lawton, Johnny Platt, Lee Wayne, "Senator" Clarke Crandall and many others.

The 1960s was still part of Chicago magic's golden age. With a booming economy, Frances's business sense, and Jay Marshall's magnetic personality, Magic, Inc. flourished. Besides books on magic, costumes and magic memorabilia, Magic, Inc. gained most of its revenue through the sale of tricks. Like musicians, magicians make a large portion of their income from live performance. But just as a songwriter makes his or her money from publishing royalties for songs they wrote that have been performed by others, magicians can invent and copyright a certain trick or gag—and then sell it to a novice, instructions included.

"During its heyday through the 1970s, the shop was running full blast," Marshall says. "At one time we had eighteen employees."

This was during the same period when Schulien's, located a few blocks south near Lincoln and Irving, continued to be a huge draw for magic fans across the country. Other places where you could catch a magic act nearby included the New York Lounge, which was located just two blocks away at Lincoln and Carmen, and the Pickle Barrel, which was located approximately one mile north on Howard and Western.

But as the shop entered the 1990s, its fortunes began to change. Clubs like the Pickle Barrel and the New York Lounge had already closed, and Schulien's was on the verge of closing as well.

"During the 1990s, the club fell on hard times," Marshall says. "Frances went into a home, and my dad ran the shop. Not only was he constantly touring but he didn't know how to run a business. Instead, he used the money he made from his shows and his position as dean of American Magicians to keep the place open, writing checks for as much as $50,000 a year to cover expenses."

Marshall died after a series of heart attacks in 2005. He is buried in the Showman's Rest Section of Woodlawn Cemetery in River Forest, Illinois, not far from the burial site where as many as sixty-five employees of the Hagenbeck-Wallace Circus who perished in a train crash in 1918 are interred. Since many of the dead were either drifters or could not be identified, many of the tombstones do not have names but merely read "Unknown Male #15" or "Unknown Female #23." The deaths of the circus elephants that died using their trunks to try to extinguish the fire have also been memorialized by large granite statues of elephants that mark the area. A man who spent his life in show business, it is both fitting and poetic that Marshall chose to be buried so close to his show business brethren. As the dean of the Society of American Magicians, Marshall's burial was accompanied by the broken wand ceremony. A tradition among magicians, it is said that his wand and his magic also perish with the magician, and thus his wand is broken in a solemn ceremony prior to his interment.

With the death of their father, it was up to Marshall's son to run Magic, Inc. Already running in the red, the institution seemed doomed. Even though the younger Marshall was an experienced magician who won the American Championship of Magic while still a teenager, his expertise was in writing award-winning TV teleplays, theatrical plays and documentaries, not retail sales. But a combination of show business, promotion and "magic" conjured up a formula to help Magic, Inc. survive. Marshall says:

> *Harry Potter saved the store. The alley in back of our magic shop is called Diagon Alley—it has been that way ever since I can remember. Well, the shop was in dire straits, almost going over. So on July 21, 2007, the seventh and final book in the Harry Potter series came out. It was called* Harry Potter and the Deathly Hallows. *The fifth movie in the series,* Harry Potter and the Order of the Phoenix, *had opened three weeks earlier. My wife* [Susan Palmer Marshall] *and I bought every Harry Potter book we could find and put them upstairs, as you could not sell the books until midnight on July 21. Right before, we handed out flyers and cards all over, even on the cars in the parking lot at Borders books. We closed shop at seven, then put on witch's and wizard's hats and opened up at nine. By nine-thirty, the place was packed. There were lines down the street both ways, the four local networks were broadcasting live, telling Chicago how to buy books at Diagon Alley. That night we stayed open until 2:00 a.m. and sold out our entire stash of Harry Potter books…and also sold quite a lot of magic. We were back in business.*

As he speaks, Marshall walks out of the theater and through the back rooms of Magic, Inc. They are filled with more posters, old stage bills and relics left from the days of his father. Behind the counter, the store's general manager, Pedro Nieves, has a deck of cards spread out over a black velvet background, demonstrating a trick to a young couple who want to purchase it so their ten-year-old son can pursue his interest in magic.

Sandy Marshall and Pedro Nieves up to their usual tricks at Magic, Inc. *Photo by author.*

Marshall looks at the counters full of books, wands, tricks and customers—almost ninety years of memories packed into a small storefront. "We are bucking the trend, as the brick and mortar magic stores are, one by one, falling by the wayside," Marshall says. "Everything is over the Internet. We even get people coming in here, checking a price, then looking at their iPhone to see if they can get it online cheaper, right in the store." Marshall laughs sarcastically, knowing that you cannot get personal service from a staff of trained magicians and over ninety years of magic history over the Internet. "But then once they buy it online, they want to come in here and have one of our expert magicians help them. Even though there might be directions, there is no 'magic' substitute for a human being standing right in front of you to show you how something works."

CHAPTER 6

RIVERVIEW MAGIC

WHAT NOSTALGIA FORGOT TO RECORD

For sixty-three years, Riverview was Chicago's permanent carnival. Opened in 1904, it was a seventy-two-acre park with over one hundred rides. Its official address was 3300 North Western, but it occupied an area ranging from the Chicago River east to Western, south to Belmont and north to Roscoe Avenue, where it ran up against the grounds of Lane Tech High School. Walk past Belmont, Western and the Chicago River during the warmer months, and the carnival would rage around you. Lights flashed and people screamed louder and louder as the Comet, the Silver Flash or the Bob's roller coaster would come catapulting forward and then gradually faded away as they went racing off into the distance. Then the slow rumble would begin to make its presence heard again, and the rattling of the wheels, the clicking of the track and the screams of the boys and girls, men and women once again filled the air with a thundering cascade as the wood and steel cars rushed onward.

On the other side of the park, the Flying Cars raced, charging upward to the stars and then falling like it was rolled off the table. The people on it were screaming, yelling, grabbing their girlfriends and boyfriends and holding their stomachs because they felt like they were bursting out of their bellies. The Ferris wheel may not have had the thrills, but as the ride rested at the crest of its climb, you would gently rock in your car and gaze over the horizon at the Chicago River, Lane Tech High School and the rooftops and chimneys of houses and cars that looked like ants moving on the road.

Riverview in its heyday. *Courtesy Tom Palozzolo.*

On the Midway, the smell of hot dogs and popcorn wafted through the thick summer air. Couples held hands and shared giant pink sticks of cotton candy, piled high and wild like a beehive hairdo. Then, it was onto the Tunnel of Love, where the sticky, sweet taste of candy was resurrected through long, slow kisses. If you were too warm, you could always cool off with the Water Bump Ride or take that same plunging, stomach-in-your-head, ears bursting plunge downward, with water spraying in your face like a giant fire hose.

"I remember approaching Riverview from the west," Tom Palozzolo, a Chicago filmmaker and historian, says. "You would be driving down Belmont, through the most normal of normal neighborhoods, and then you would go over a bridge and all of a sudden you would see the Bob's and roller coasters and Aladdin's Castle—it was like this magic world just suddenly appeared."

Yet behind the laughter, flashing lights, organ music, smiling faces, aw shucks, golly gee, what the heck let's jump on the coaster again nostalgia there was another side of Riverview. Underneath the rides, behind the high walls of Aladdin's Castle and inside the dark canvas tent was a world where people gawked at the fire eaters and watched with eyes wide open as dancers did the hootchie-cootchie. This was called the carnival sideshow.

"There was an area not far from the Western Avenue entrance and the Bobs, not far from the Midway—it was the sideshow or freak show," Palozzolo says. "I think it my have cost an extra fifty cents. It seemed sort of dark and dingy but interesting, and when you went there, you felt like you were seeing something that a lot of people didn't know about."

Along with the fire eaters and dancers, many magicians, with their dark suits, disappearing cards and women who were sawed in half, were a big part of the inner world of Riverview. One of these magicians was Anthony Coulter, known as "Tony Marks, the Aristocrat of Deception." During his career, this Chicago native appeared with such performers as Sammy Davis Jr. and Liberace. He eventually made it to the *Ed Sullivan Show* and the London Palladium. While in London, he even gave a command performance for Queen Elizabeth in 1959. But it was underneath the flashing lights and roaring rides at Riverview where Coulter learned his craft.

"I first got interested in magic when I saw a magician performing at Riverview," Coulter says. "That was one of the places a kid could be exposed to magic, and after that, I ran to the nearest local magic shop. The rest, as they say, is history."

Another magician who got his start at Riverview was Anthony Thompson. According to the Chicago Map of Magic, Thompson grew up in Chicago's Old Town neighborhood at 1629 North Hudson, not far from St. Michael's Church. Riverview was just a short ride northwest, and at the age of thirteen, Thompson began working at Riverview as a sword swallower and fire eater. It was here that he learned not only magic but also the ins and outs of show business. So much so that, although he was in great demand as a magician, he also worked setting up shows for Penn and Teller and Lance Burton. Thompson also went on to have a feature role in the film *The Aristocrats*.

Marshall Brodien, the man who brought magic into the television age through his invention of TV Magic Cards and portrayal as Wizzo on *Bozo's Circus*, also got his start at Riverview. In his book, *The Magical Life of Marshall Brodien*, he talks of tricks, including simple tabletop magic like the Chinese sticks. A standard of magicians then and now, it consists of two short bamboo rods with shiny cloths attached to strings at both ends that seem to move magically and independently without pulleys. Another standard trick he performed was the egg bag, where a wooden egg appears and disappears from a small black velvet sack.

Larger tricks included the Gufus plant, a plant that refuses to grow until the end, when flowers bloom so quickly they spring at the audience like snakes. The pillory escape trick consisted of a young girl tied to a wooden post by many different ropes. Yet when the magician gives the command, the ropes suddenly unravel themselves, and the girl walks away from her bondage. Brodien added the extra enticement of promising, "If the girl does not walk away in three seconds, everybody will get a free ticket to the show."

There was also the blade box, a standard trick for many magicians. An audience member is first picked out and tests the firmness and sharpness of the blades. Convinced that they are genuine, magicians like Brodien then ensconce a person, usually a beautiful young assistant, into a coffin-like box. Dozens of razor sharp blades are plunged into it. How could the woman survive what looked like certain death?

Brodien and the Riverview magical staff added another attraction to the magic. Instead of a "normal" beautiful young girl, "Sepintina the Snake Girl" stepped inside the box. A

The Tattooed Lady, part of the ambiance at Riverview. *Photo by Tom Palozzolo.*

woman who could "shape her body and skin into that of a snake," she was also wearing a sheer robe. Magicians were often a mere warm up act for these odd human performers, sometimes referred to as "carnival freaks," in Chicago's world of magic and mojo. In most cases, curiosity about the girl, the magic and the sheer robe overcame the financial reservations of many. Brodien and other magicians often worked as the men whose job it was to get the attention of those willing to shell out an extra quarter or dollar to see these acts. Their intended customers often included the rube from the country, the curious suburbanite and, most notably, the innocent boy titillated enough to spend his last dime or quarter saved for a hot dog luncheon on mysteries beyond his boyhood mind. On hot summer days and into the chilly fall, Brodien lured them with his carnie barker spiel:

You'll see Priscilla the Monkey Girl with long, black, shaggy hair just like a monkey...two rows of teeth in the upper jaw like the anthropoid ape with pouches on her side where she can store food for days at a time. She is Married to Emmet the Alligator-skinned man covered from his head to the toes of his feet with rough, tough, corrugated hide laid out in checks and squares like that of a crocodile...His skin so rough and tough that you couldn't penetrate it with the sharpest of knives...sheds his skin twice a year like a crocodile... On a hot day he keeps his body moist in cold water...You'll see Grace M Daniels the mule faced woman, with the head face, and characteristics of a giant, Georgia mule. When she removes her heavy, black veil—not to be vulgar because you can't see through the material—and you'll see in the flesh not something that is stuffed, mummified, made of wax, or made up for the occasion to fool you, but created by the hand of God, born of a human mother the same as you or I...a sight you'll go away talking about for the longest day you live...something your mother has never seen.

Throughout the hot days and warm nights, Brodien and countless other Riverview sideshow barkers would continue to bring in the crowds and stand at the edge of the tent, advertising more acts and more amazing sights like Tiny Carter, the World's Fattest Man, Americo, the Atomical Wonder and countless sword swallowers, fire eaters, knife throwers and animals from midget horses to five-legged cows.

"I remember a guy whose eyes would pop out of his head called Popeye, or a woman who would put a light bulb in her mouth, and when she would stand up on this box, a current would come on and the light bulb lit up," Palozzolo says. "There were also a lot of tattooed people and contortionists. One old guy wore a long overcoat, and he would somehow move his head around and around until it moved 360 degrees and you could see the back of it coming out of his trench coat.'

Like magicians, they lived in a different world, a world of constant performances, months on the road and the constant pressure to perform. Yet while most magicians could look forward to returning to a home, family and "normal life," their sideshow brethren often could not walk down the streets without causing a freakish stir.

"These are people who had no other options," says Glen C. Davies, a former circus employee and muralist who paints in the tradition of the circus sideshow banners. "At home, they were objects of shame left in windowless attics. But in the circus, they were part of the circus and carnival family. They were treated with respect and dignity by the other performers, traveled and

The ruins of Riverview. *Photo by Tom Palozzolo.*

made good money. They were not exploited but, like actors or magicians, were very much in charge of their own performances."

Riverview closed for good in 1968, the victim of television, suburbanization and the automobile culture. Today, a shopping mall and DeVry Technical Institute stand on much of the land once occupied by the park. In back of the school, running along the eastern edge of the Chicago River, there still sits a tract of land covered with trees, weeds and a makeshift bicycle motocross course fashioned by local youths. Wildlife in the form of squirrels, raccoons and even an occasional fox, coyote or rooster has also made homes for themselves in this area. Yet like Riverview itself, if you look beneath the surface, you will find a mysterious world. In this case, it is the remnants of the park, long forgotten and buried beneath the sands of time, which had run for almost fifty years. Half cylinders of cement, which may have been part of one of the park's many canals, still sit in the park's west end, near the river. Large chunks of exposed stone, perhaps the base of one of the park's many rides, lay exposed to the surface. Digging just beneath the surface, you see what could well have been the cement foundations of the smaller structures, perhaps a food stand, bathroom or storage shed, buried beneath the leaves and dirt. Sitting in this area on a warm summer's day, it is not hard to close your eyes and hear the clackety clack of the wooden roller coasters, the clanging gears of the bumper cars and the voice of a magician bellowing out, "Go ahead and check the blade, I assure you it is not hollow, nor plastic, but stainless steel, sharpened to the point of a tiger's tooth…"

CHAPTER 7

CHICAGO'S GOLDEN AGE
OF MAGIC

Downtown Chicago in the 1940s and '50s was a world upon itself. Men dressed in suits and hats, and women with their newest dresses, bonnets and handbags poured off streetcars, electric buses, up from the subway, down from the El and in and out of cars and cabs. Like waves on Lake Michigan, pedestrians surged up and down State and Randolph Streets, Michigan, Wabash and Madison Avenues; the flood of people subsided temporarily with a changing stoplight, only to fill the streets once the light had changed. Many were there to work, but people were also there to eat lunch or shop in stores like Marshall Field's, Carson's, Sears, Montgomery Wards, Wieboldt's and hundreds of other large stores and smaller specialty shops.

After the sun went down, the Loop and Near North were lit by neon signs. Sometimes three stories high, they flashed pink, yellow, green, red, orange and purple, their colors reflecting on the wet city sidewalks. They told the people that they were now entering a different world, a world of restaurants like the Blackhawk Restaurant, theaters like the Blackstone and Schubert and nightclubs like the Chez Paree and Fritzel's. Chicago was also filled with magic, not only in downtown magic shops but also in hotel theaters, nightclubs, bars and restaurants throughout downtown and the rest of the city streets.

"During that time, you could see, learn about or experience magic pretty much twenty-four hours a day, seven days a week," Eugene Burger says.

Burger has been heralded as Chicago's Best Magician by *New City* and *Chicago Magazine*, awarded the Merlin Award by the International Magicians

Left: Jay Marshall represented the Golden Age of Magic as much as any performer. *Courtesy Sandy and Susan Marshall Collection.*

Below: Frank Everhart performing at Chicago's Ivanhoe Theater in the late 1950s. *Courtesy Sandy and Susan Marshall Collection.*

Society and named as one of the One Hundred Most Influential Magicians of the Twentieth Century by *MAGIC Magazine*. A native of Chicago's Portage Park Neighborhood, Burger has lived in Chicago during part or all of eight decades and credits the city's "magical" environment for much of his interest in magic and his continued success.

> *I remember when I was a boy I would take the Milwaukee bus to the train at Logan Square and then get off near Randolph and Dearborn. Right there, within three blocks, were three magic stores: Ireland's (109 North Dearborn), Joe Berg (30 West Washington and later 36 West Randolph) and Abbott's (54 West Randolph). To show the interest that there was in magic, none of them were at street level and none of them really had any visible advertising. Joe Berg's was on the second floor, just a regular shop surrounded by small offices and places like that. When you walked in, a little bell would go off. The great magician Okito worked there, so they specialized in Asian stuff, but Joe was a great guy. Ireland's was run by Frances Ireland, who was a brilliant author and magician. Abbott's Magic was in the same building as the Woods Theater (designed by Louis Sullivan) before they tore it down, and as I remember, Jack Gould manned the counter for quite a while.*

But these were not the only locations in downtown Chicago.

> *You also had the National Magic Company, which was on the mezzanine level of the Palmer House Hotel, but it was not in a high-traffic area, it was way in the back. I remember all they had was a sign that said NATIONAL MAGIC in smoked glass. Pretty much everything there was nickel plated, as you had a lot of items from Germany and Italy. One other place downtown was the Treasure Chest. It was also located near Randolph and Dearborn. That shop had big windows facing the street that attracted lots of tourists. A lot of the space was devoted to pinball and other kinds of arcade games, but there was a large magic counter as well. Upstairs they had a pro shop. They just didn't let anybody up there. It was manned by different people. I think Don Allen ran it for a while. I remember one day, Don opened it just for us. He sold me a miniature French guillotine.*

Known for his long gray beard, Burger has been called everything from "Mr. Beard" to being compared with Gandolph the Wizard from J.R.R. Tolkien's *Lord of the Rings* trilogy. He has lectured nationally and internationally on magic and twice has been named Lecturer of the Year at the Magic Castle. Besides being called "Perhaps Chicago's Most Eminent Magician" in *New City* and "One of the Best Close-Up Magicians in the Country" by the *Chicago Tribune,* Burger has been featured on *The Art of Magic* on PBS and *Mysteries of Magic* on the Learning Channel. He's been profiled twice on CNN, and *Genii Magazine* stated, "For decades, Eugene Burger has been recognized by magicians and the public as being one of the finest magicians alive."

Burger credits much of his success to his parents, who took him downtown and later throughout the city to buy magic equipment and see magicians perform. But he also credits much of it to the virtues and values of what now seems to be a lost era when personalities that you could see, feel, hear and touch manned the magic shops. Not only were these people real experts, but they seemed to care as well. He says:

> *I can't cite enough how important it was for me as a young man and magician, the inspiration and guidance I got from the people who manned the magic shops. I remember I would walk into Joe Berg with, say, thirty-five bucks saved up from gifts and birthdays. By this time, even though I was young, I had been coming to the magic stores for a while, so they knew me. I would pick five tricks or magical items off the shelf, and they would tell me, "The first one won't work for you; the second one will; three, four and five, no, no, no." So I would end up spending less money than I intended, because they cared. Caring and guidance is something you can't find on TV or on the Internet, and it was this personal attention and care that made Eugene Burger the magician.*

Besides the many magic shops, Chicago's downtown also had another magical landmark. While Hollywood may have had movie stars who gathered for luncheons at the Brown Derby, or New York's Broadway had Toffenetti's, there was one luncheon spot that personified the feeling, attitude and camaraderie of the Golden Age of Magic in Chicago. Called the Magician's Roundtable, the tradition began at De Lazon's Restaurant at 127 North Dearborn. Its heyday was at Drake's Restaurant. Today, you may tweet or e-mail, but during the Golden Age of Magic, the great ones met in person to not only eat lunch and enjoy cocktails but also share secrets of magic and life itself.

Just as many of Chicago's downtown stores and lunch counters went to sleep for the night and were replaced by bars and clubs, the world of magic was also

The Magician's Roundtable at Chicago's Drake's Restaurant, a true symbol of the Golden Age of Magic in Chicago. *Courtesy Sandy and Susan Marshall Collection.*

Sandy Marshall's prize membership card for the Magician's Roundtable. *Courtesy Sandy and Susan Marshall Collection.*

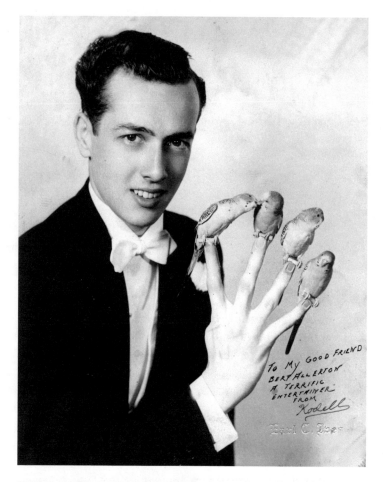

In 1941, Jack Kodell moved to Chicago, where he created "A Fantasy of Birds." At the 1947 International Magic Convention, he was hailed by Chicago native Harry Blackstone Sr. as "the boy who has revolutionized magic." *Courtesy Tom Palozzolo.*

transformed. But like flashing neon, the stars and the moon, magic glistens, glows and radiates at night. Always mysterious, the magicians in their dark top hats with their glistening white doves and vanishing cards are conjured with far more effect once dark shadows take over the streets.

The Empire Room at the Palmer House Hotel (17 East Monroe) featured magicians like Cardini, who also appeared at the Chicago Theater. The Gaslight Club, famous for its waitresses and their low-cut, Moulin Rouge–style attire, also featured magicians Alton Sharpe and Robert Parrish.

"Back then you could see top-flight magic in Chicago any night of the week," Burger says. "Downtown you had John Platt at the Gay 90's at the La Salle Hotel, Burt Allerton at the Pump Room, magicians performing at the Empire Room at the Palmer House and Dix and Norb's Magic Inn just west of the Loop."

Even though Chicago was centered downtown, there were also many historic landmarks located outside the Loop. One of these was the Edgewater Beach Hotel. Built in 1916, it was located on the shores of Lake Michigan near Foster Avenue. Built in a pink, semi–Art Deco style, it rivaled the great hotels of Hollywood and Miami, attracting stars like Frank Sinatra, Judy Garland, Glenn Miller and Artie Shaw and Presidents Roosevelt and Eisenhower. Also appearing there were many magicians as either main or opening acts. Also along Chicago's lakefront at Broadway and Wellington, the Ivanhoe Theater was the site for the premiere of one of Tennessee Williams's final plays. Its stage held stars like Jessica Tandy, Piper Laurie and Christopher Walken and many magicians.

"Frank Eberhardt and Lee Le Roi performed regularly at the Ivanhoe's Black Night Bar; Marshall Brodien was a regular at the Cairo Club at Sheridan and Foster. Brodien also performed at the Magic Lounge, but that was really the home of Clark (known to all as Senator) Crandall," recalls Burger.

Known for his dark glasses and handlebar mustache, Crandall was famous for his one-liners and ability to verbally put anybody in their place. Crandall was also known for the dice-stacking trick, in which four separate dice were placed in a giant cup. After the cup was shaken, one giant die was in their place.

Crandall, in turn, got the Magic Lounge job from magician Johnny Paul. At first, it was Paul who established the regular show of magic at the lounge. The establishment was located in Cicero, a place that first gained infamy as Al Capone's headquarters when things got a little too hot in Chicago in the late 1920s. After Capone's conviction for tax evasion in 1932, Cicero remained a "mob town" where gambling, prostitution and other vices were as transparent as the negligees worn by the girls in the strip clubs. Like musicians, gangsters and magicians had some things in common. Both were more or less creatures of the night who exchanged the nine-to-five grind for evenings in clubs; gangsters from Al Capone, who employed Max Malini, to Sam Giancana enjoyed the diversions that magicians provided. Occasionally, however, spending time around gangsters proved not to be the safest way to make a living.

"Legend has it that one night Paul was standing out in the alley in back of the Cairo Club, taking a breather, when he saw something that he wasn't supposed to see," Burger says. "Next thing you know, he moved to Las Vegas, and nobody really saw him around Chicago again."

As the night grows darker and the neon flashes brighter, magic, music and the occasional inclusion of alcohol also played a part in the Golden Age of Magic. After all, the 1940s, '50s and early '60s was the era of the martini, Manhattan and gin rickey cocktail. Many were consumed while watching magicians perform at Chicago's great clubs, but there was one place where magicians and their fans seemed to always end up.

"During that era," Burger says, "when it was really late at night, the place you took your girlfriend at two and didn't leave until four in the morning was the New York Lounge." Located near Foster and Lincoln, not far from Chicago's magic base, Magic, Inc., the New York Lounge was owned by Mike Pappas. As Burger said, it was the late-night, and often the last, stop for not only magicians but also many Chicagoans touring the bars. Just as cable television sometimes relaxes standards in the wee hours of the morning, so did the New York Lounge. Often, the magic and jokes got a little risqué. Jay Marshall was known to add a bit of this type of humor to his act, but even the former dean of magicians concedes some of this territory to magician Heba Haba Al Andrucci, who not only crossed the line but danced on top of it. Marshall, who was also known for having one of the most risqué acts in all of magic, said:

> *Heba Haba's trademark trick usually involved a sugar cube and a pretty woman. He'd ask the lady her name and then take the cube, draw a letter on it with a pencil and, say her name was Laurie, draw the letter L. Then he'd drop it in a glass of water and tell you to put her hand over the glass. When it dissolved, you'd lift your hand and there would be the L on your palm. Then it would move to the back of her hand. Then he'd say, "There is one on your hip too. You better go look." So she'd go into the ladies' room, and he had a microphone at the bar with a speaker hooked up to there and he'd announce, with the whole crowd hearing, "No, no. Look a little higher."*

Although Magic, Inc. and the many magic shops prospered during this era, one establishment became not only a local legend but also famous nationally and internationally as the home of great food and close-up magic: Schulien's Restaurant.

CHAPTER 8

SCHULIEN'S

AMERICA'S GREATEST MAGIC RESTAURANT

It's five o'clock on a Friday night in Chicago, circa 1962. Men in snap-brimmed hats, wearing dark suits with narrow ties, begin to file into Schulien's. Soon, cold beers, Manhattans and martinis begin to flow from behind the bar. One man is sipping on a cold bottle of Schlitz as he sits underneath the yellowing newspaper headlines and black-and-white photos of stars from stage, screen and vaudeville that line the walls. He is approached by Charlie Schulien, the bar's owner. A heavy-set, jovial man, he spreads a deck of cards out on the dark oak table.

"Now, I want you to pick a card out of the deck," he says, reaching into his shirt pocket, "and take this pen and sign it."

The man picks up a ballpoint pen and scribbles his name on a card, which Schulien quickly places in the middle of the deck.

"See this tack," Schulien says. "I am going to stick it in the deck."

Schulien takes out a white thumbtack and, with his thick fingers, presses it firmly into the deck of cards. Then he heaves the entire deck into the air. Cards cascade upward and then fall downward, the black and red spades, clubs, diamonds and hearts flickering in the bar's dim light. Soon, the floor is littered with fifty-one cards. Yet, as you look up at the ceiling, one card, the one that the man signed and selected, is mysteriously tacked to the wall.

Stunned, the customer, looks down, takes a long sip of beer and looks back again at the card on the wall. He then lifts his hat, scratches his head and says, "How did you do that?"

This is a question that has been asked at Schulien's, and now O'Donovan's, for over seventy-five years. During this time, it has been a performance space, laboratory and general hangout for magicians including Harry Blackstone Sr., Jay Marshall, Marshall Brodien, Harry Blackstone Jr., David Copperfield, Penn of Penn and Teller and many others. The restaurant's owners, Matt and later Charlie Schulien, became renowned magicians in their own right. Other performers like Don Allen, Mike Krzak and Al Andrucci, forever known as "Heba Haba Al" for his trademark variation of "hocus pocus," became local celebrities. Al James, who has been performing at Schulien's since the final days of the Golden Age of Magic, carries on the tradition. James performs at the restaurant every weekend, throwing down cards that change and reappear and performing other versions of what James refers to as "tableside magic."

"Schulien's was one of the establishments that perfected this type of magic," James says as he opens a small duffel bag filled with decks of cards, baseballs and other props used in his act. "You are working at a restaurant, and you know that people are eating, drinking, and that other customers or a server is going to come by any minute. So you can't do anything elaborate

Above: What a golden age! Matt Schulien (left), Jay Marshall (center) and a third magician at Schulien's. *Courtesy Sandy and Susan Marshall Collection.*

Opposite: Matt Schulien performs close-up magic at the restaurant he made famous. *Courtesy Sandy and Susan Marshall Collection.*

like levitations or something that requires staging or setup. Instead," he continues breaking the seal on a deck of cards, "the tricks have to be short and fast, and everything pretty much has to be done in a ten-minute span."

Although the acts may take ten minutes, they have helped this Chicago entertainment entity survive for over a century. The story began in 1888, immediately following the Great Chicago Fire. At that time, the city was booming, with the population growing at an astounding rate. Statistics from the U.S. Census show that in 1880, Chicago had approximately 503,185 people. This nearly doubled in 1890, as the city grew to 1,099,850. By 1910, the number more than doubled again, as the number of citizens was reported at 2,185,283. Many of the new residents during this period were German and Irish immigrants. These immigrants brought with them many of the traditions from their old country, including a culture of dining, socializing and politics that centered on the consumption of beer. Many of Chicago's city fathers and founding leaders, including William Ogden, Michael Diversey, Conrad Sulzer and Charles Wacker, made their fortunes selling beer. Joseph Schulien had been a driver for a Milwaukee brewery called Schlitz. As part of what became a long battle for territory, he bought a pub called Quincy No. 9 for Schlitz in order to prevent it from being bought by a rival brewer.

In 1918, they moved the bar to 1800 North Halsted, in a building that now houses the Black Duck Tavern and Grill. Family members say that during Prohibition, Schulien's became a speakeasy with liquor supplied by Al Capone. As Chicago's German American population moved north, so, too, did Schulien's, as in 1948, the bar moved to its present location (now named O' Donavan's) at 2100 West Irving Park Road. In order to service the neighborhood, the bar started serving food. Not just food but hearty German fare, including roast duck, short ribs, wienerschnitzel, planked whitefish and German chocolate cake. But as in the case with establishments like Resi's Beer Stube and Lashet's Inn, which still inhabit the same block today, food and drink were not enough to bring in a steady supply of customers. Then, suddenly, something appeared on the horizon that made Schulien's not only famous throughout Chicagoland but across the nation—magic. James says:

> *The tradition of magic started when, one night, Harry Blackstone Sr. came in for dinner. He was a big celebrity then, and Matt Schulien, who was a young boy, was really excited, and Blackstone was kind enough to teach him magic tricks. He [Schulien] did take some lessons from a local magician, but he pretty much picked things up on his own…Soon it became more than a hobby. He started doing tricks for customers. This became popular, and*

people started to identify it with the club, so much so that he had to hire other magicians like Don Allen, who was on the Tonight Show *several times, Heba Haba Al and Jimmy Krzak, who worked here for eighteen years. At one time, it was so busy that on weekends we had three magicians.*

Matt Schulien died in a plane crash in 1959, but the business and the magic were continued by his sons Ed and Charlie. They continued the tradition of magic, and soon Schulien's became known nationally. In 1979, Charlie Schulien appeared in a Schlitz beer commercial with his son, Robert, as part of a national ad campaign that featured Chicago magic. The bar was also the subject of stories in *Life* magazine, NBC's *Today Show* and dozens of local news and TV segments, including two featuring Harry Blackstone Jr. and David Copperfield.

James has been working at Schulien's/O'Donovan's since 1978. After almost forty years, he has not lost his excitement for the job or the thrill of magic, especially the surprised look on the face of a customer when a card, baseball or simple object disappears and reappears or is transformed before his very eyes.

"My interest in magic started when I was eight, when my aunt gave me a magic set." James, who grew up in Cleveland, says. "Then, a short time later, there was a magician in a settlement house, which is kind of like the park district in Cleveland. So between the magic set and the magician, they definitely got me going."

After leaving home, James worked as a radio disc jockey in Cleveland. "It was a middle-of-the-road station," James says. "We played a lot of Frank Sinatra and Tony Bennett."

After that he got a job with the Corey Company, which brought him to Chicago, but the company went out of business and James was out of a job. He says:

Before that, for the last couple of years I had been going to Schulien's or to the Pickle Barrel to watch Heba Haba Al. One night, Heba Haba slipped on a pat of butter and broke his shoulder, and they asked me to fill in at Pickle Barrel for six weeks. During that time, I got to know the guys at New York Lounge and worked there for a while. Then I got an offer to go to the Ivanhoe, which was a major theater venue, so I went there. I never had a teacher, but working at places like the Pickle Barrel, I picked up what I needed, at least to get started.

James's greatest feat of magic at Schulien's may have been his reenactment of Houdini's famous milk can escape. "For publicity, I did the milk can escape, where you basically escape out of a large metal can that they used to transport milk in," James says. "Houdini invented it, and we were looking for something to do to commemorate Houdini's birthday, which was on April 6."

The milk can escape was, for a time, Houdini's most popular attraction. Advertised with orange and blue posters that proclaimed "Failure Means a Drowning Death," Houdini squeezed himself into a large steel milk can as stagehands filled it with as many as twenty buckets of water. When he did the trick, Houdini would ask spectators if they cared to put themselves into the can (with the lid off) and try to hold their breath. Almost all emerged gasping after less than a minute. As a safety measure, and to up the visual ante of potential danger, Houdini's assistant, Kukol, would stand over the can with an axe, asking the audience if they thought it was time to "hack."

Some seventy-five years later, the same type of precaution was also taken by James.

"If it was a magic trick it would be okay to fail, but an escape, you have to be very cautious and careful," James says. "I had a magician named Jim Summers coach me as well as stand by. To be safe," James continues, "the first few times you don't lock it. Then you do it without water, and then add water. The last step is to add water, and finally you lock it. It is a gradual process. There is danger involved, so if you are not 100 percent sure, don't do it."

As customers begin to file into O'Donovan's, James recounts more details of one of the most daring magical acts in the history of Schulien's.

I did it on April 6, 1980. I began practicing on April 5, and it was unusually hot, ninety degrees. I was in the backyard in a swimsuit. I was in and out of the can, and it was great. On the day of the event, however, it was forty-five degrees. So we had to get hot water from inside the restaurant. After we filled it up with water, I had a policeman put on a lid on and then added padlocks. A large curtain was raised. Then I got in the milk can and put on the handcuffs.

Reporters from Chicago's major newspapers, as well as WBBM TV, were there to record the event. An overflow crowd in the parking lot and bar and cars slowing to a stop along Chicago's Irving Park Road also looked on as James sat inside the confined, dark can trying to free himself from the handcuffs. Time passed, and the audience began to look at their watches. After a minute, many began shifting and placing their hands on their foreheads. Finally, after almost

Al James is still wowing the crowd with his close-up magic at O'Donovan's. *Photo by author.*

two minutes, they began gasping. A short time later, the curtain was raised, and James emerged, soaking wet, cold and exhausted.

Most of the time, however, the performances at Schulien's were not as dangerous or dramatic. Besides speed, one thing that many magicians used to compensate the lack of props and staging was humor. Thus, it was not only the food and the magic but also the oversized personalities of the stocky Schulien clan that spread the establishment's fame well beyond the neighbor or worker looking for a beer and schnitzel.

"A lot of politicians have come in here over the years. Mayor Richard M. Daley; Governor Thompson, who had me do magic for a young daughter; Governor Ogilvie, who came in here at least once a month," James says. "Of course, a lot of sports stars or people who were associated with the Cubs. Harry Carey used to come in here all the time. Not only before or after games but during the off-season as well."

Another famous Cub announcer, and member of Baseball's Hall of Fame, visited Schulien's even more often and for a longer period than any of the players of Carey. "This place was practically a home base for a lot of the people who worked at WGN and especially my husband," Patricia "Pat" Brickhouse, widow of the legendary announcer Jack Brickhouse, says. "Jack was a kid at heart. He was fascinated by magic, and so was I. Eventually I became fascinated too, and we would sit here for hours listening and watching Al, who worked here five days a week," Brickhouse says.

When Schulien's moved in 1947, the neighborhood was a staunch German-Irish stronghold centered on St. Benjamin's Church. Known as North-Center or St. Ben's, the area held up well during the suburban flight of the 1960s due to the close-knit ethnic community. The area deteriorated a bit during the late 1970s and '80s but then experienced a great upsurge of urban renewal in the 1990s as young urban professionals (yuppies) began buying and rehabbing the three-flats and frame houses that lined the surrounding blocks. Unfortunately, Schulien's was not able to experience this urban renaissance. Brother Ed had dropped out of the business full time to sell real estate, and after over 110 years, Schulien's ended its reign as Chicago's longest continually operating tavern, closing its doors in 1999.

"Charlie died while he was trying to sell it," James says. "Those were traumatic years. I thought it was all over, so I went to California to perform at [Los Angeles's most prestigious magic club,] the Magic Castle."

According to Sean Parnell's book and website *The Chicago Bar Project*, Schulien's was sold to the owners of the Twisted Lizard in Lincoln Park and then transformed into the Irving Ale House for a short stint prior to becoming O'Donovan's.

"In the meantime, the old customers were coming in, asking, 'Where is the magic?'" James says. "Well, they didn't want to lose the old customers. One day, I was eating lunch at a restaurant, Lashet's across the street, and they said, 'Hey Al, they've been looking for you.'"

O'Donovan's, with its outdoor seating, magnificent summer patio and mix of classic rock and contemporary hits piped through the sound system, is a far cry from the Sinatra/Bennett days of the 1960s and '70s. Gone, too, are the

O'Donovan's and James preserving the magic and history of Schulien's. *Photo by author.*

schnitzels, red cabbage and short ribs, replaced by wings, nachos and grilled fish, chicken and burgers. Yet while James spends his nights making baseballs, cards and other objects disappear, the magic itself has not vanished.

"Schulien's has had the longest-running magic performances of any place in Chicago," Brickhouse says. "It kept on going after Matt [Schulien] died and the kids took over, survived changes in the neighborhood, the changeover from live acts to television. So," she says, staring at the wood-paneled walls, "when most people thought of magic in Chicago, they thought of Schulien's. Magic is part of the tradition of the establishment, so why change it?"

CHAPTER 9

MARSHALL BRODIEN

RIVERVIEW, *BOZO'S CIRCUS* AND TV MAGIC CARDS

Marshall Brodien may be best known for portraying the lovable clown "Wizzo the Wizard" on WGN Chicago's *Bozo's Circus* for over two decades. Some may also know him as the inventor and marketer of the million-selling TV Magic Cards, which introduced magic to tens of thousands of children in the 1960s and '70s. Yet Brodien began his magic career at Chicago's famous Riverview Park and also witnessed, participated in and was perhaps the most famous product of Chicago's Golden Age of Magic.

Marshall Brodien was born on Chicago's North Side, where he attended Louisa May Alcott Elementary School, the same grammar school as the author. His interest in magic began when he first walked into a magic shop located on North Clark Street, next to the old Parkway Theater. At the age of fifteen, Brodien's interest in school waned, and he began working as a demonstrator at the Treasure Chest at 19 West Randolph. There he not only learned magic skills but also had the opportunity to learn from some of magic's greats, like Don Allen and Theodore Bamberg, aka Okito.

At the age of seventeen, Brodien got a job at Chicago's Riverview Park. As chronicled in the "Riverview" portion of the book, he worked as a carnie barker, magician and freak show host. While working with performers like Sword Swallower Tony Marino, he learned two other skills: sword swallowing and fire eating.

He worked summers at Riverview and the rest of the year at the Treasure Chest, and by the time he was nineteen, Brodien was already seasoned enough to start working at a famous magic shop from Chicago's Golden Age of Magic, the Magic Lounge. The club was the home base of one of Chicago's most legendary magicians, Clarke Crandall, also known as "The Senator." It was also located in Cicero, Illinois. The former home base of Al Capone, Cicero was a wide-open town. In the days before Las Vegas, it was Chicago's own little sin city, where strip clubs, gambling and other forms of vice were freely available. The Magic Lounge itself was surrounded by establishments like the Towne Hotel, which used to be Al Capone's headquarters; the Rainbow Lounge, allegedly owned and operated by Al Capone's brother; and the 4811, where women danced totally nude. Mobsters like Joey Aiuppa and Jackie Cerone regularly frequented the place.

During one of his first weeks at the Magic Lounge, Brodien performed the vanishing birdcage trick for a short man with a dark suit and fedora whom the locals referred to as "Gumpy." As told in his biography, *The Magical Life of Marshall Brodien*, Brodien apparently told Gumpy to tap the birdcage three times and then a bird would appear. After doing so, nothing happened, and Gumpy replied, "There's no friggin boid in there."

He tried again, to no avail, but Brodien made the cage disappear. Disappointed, Gumpy asked his friend how Brodien did it, to which he answered, "I don't know; the kid's a magician, it's magic."

Gumpy was not satisfied with the answer. He pointed to Brodien: "Hey you, Gumpy wants to know where the cage went to."

Brodien answered that it was a magical secret. Apparently, Gumpy was not happy with the answer, as he proceeded to pull out a large caliber handgun and point it at Brodien, saying, "Like I was sayin, where's dat friggin boidcage?"

It was at this point that Brodien produced the birdcage from up his sleeve. Gumpy was happy, and Brodien learned that the magician's code of not revealing your secrets had exceptions—one of them being a gun pointed at your head.

After a stint in the army where Brodien was quickly relived of his duties peeling potatoes and standing guard in favor of performing first for lieutenants and captains and then colonels and generals, Brodien returned home to Chicago. It was the 1950s, still the heyday of the Golden Age of Magic in Chicago. Brodien got a job headlining at the Boston Nocturne Nightclub at 4224 West North Avenue. At the time, pamphlets for the city advertized him competing against the likes of Johnny Mathis at the Chez Paree and the Harmonicats. Now a headliner, Brodien decided he needed a new angle to his act. Hypnosis was a technique employed by magicians ranging from Houdini to today's Neil Tobin. He also traveled back along the carnie circuit to Texas, where he learned/purchased a magic trick called the broomstick suspension. Invented by Robert Houdin in the 1840s, suspension or levitation is still a staple of magic acts today. Thus, armed with his new "bag of tricks," Brodien was able to attract customers to the club. Located near the intersections of Grand Avenue, North Avenue and Kostner Avenue, it was off the beaten path of Chicago's downtown magic clubs and shops, as well as establishments like Magic, Inc., Schulien's and the New York Lounge, which were located in Chicago's North Center "magic district." Nevertheless, Brodien was able to pull in customers as well as reporters, such as one for the *Chicago American* who wrote of Brodien's act:

> *Marshall Brodien, magician and hypnotist at the Boston Nocturne Club on the northwest side, performs one of the most amazing allusions* [sic] *ever done by any magician. He hypnotizes his lovely assistant Evelyn so that she is stiff and rigid and then places her atop the sweeping end of a broom, where she remains suspended in space. It's a real fooler, and when we asked Brodien how it's done he said, "Tell your readers to come and see the show and maybe I'll explain it."*

In 1961, Brodien moved closer to Chicago's lakefront and the magic district, getting a job at the Cairo Supper Club. Here, his hypnotic skills increased to the point where one volunteer was apparently under a lot of stress—so much so that when the song "Night Train" began playing, he jumped up on stage and began dancing furiously. He also "let loose" in another way. At first patrons thought that the stains on his pants were from a spilled drink, but men in the washroom reported that when he heard the song, he ran away from the urinal before he had finished using it.

Another man, apparently out of his trance, left the club and began driving down Irving Park Road. The Chicago police spotted him weaving and acting strangely, almost as if he was "in a trance." When the police took him back to the Cairo Supper Club, Brodien and the audience corroborated that he was hypnotized and not intoxicated.

His success at the Cairo Club earned him press citywide, as well as a thoughtful blurb by Jay Marshall for the magazine *Rogue* entitled "Chicago, Magic City," in which the fellow magician complimented Brodien for the speed and success of his hypnosis. Press like this also helped to launch Brodien on the most successful run of his career as Wizzo the Wizard on *Bozo's Circus*.

Bozo's Circus, also known as *The Bozo Show*, was the most successful local children's television show in the nation. It ran for more than forty years. During its peak of popularity, it was aired via satellite around the nation and the world. Locally, people had to wait as long as seven years for tickets to the show. Ironically, WGN studio is located near Addison and Western, four blocks north of Riverview, Brodien's first place of employment and another legendary Chicago magic location. During the early 1960s, Brodien had appeared on the show off and on, often performing magic, but his performance schedule at trade shows, theaters and nightclubs precluded him from a regular stint. Then one day he put together a costume. Inspired by the Arabian Nights, it featured a large pendant, a turban, a black handlebar mustache and goatee and a genie-like tunic.

He recalls, "One day, after I rolled my eyes, which always made the audience laugh, I just happened to say, 'Doody doody do,' and they laughed harder."

From that point on, a local TV legend was born. Say, "Doody doody do" to almost anyone who lived in Chicagoland during the 1960s, '70s and '80s, and their faces will light up. Brodien often accompanied each "doody do" with a disappearing coin, all stemming from his magical Stone of Zanzibar. In the 1970s, Ned Locke, known as Ringmaster Ned, retired and was replaced by Frazier Thomas, former host of *Garfield Goose*. In the 1980s, Bob Bell retired as Bozo, but the show rolled on. Finally, in 1993, Roy Brown, "Cooky the Cook," retired for health reasons, and in 1993, Brodien left as well. *The Bozo Show* continued in various stages until 2001, when WGN produced a final special, *Bozo: 40 Years of Fun*. Brodien returned for the final taping, but by this time, he had moved on from Bozo. Today, his Wizzo costume is on permanent display at Chicago's Museum of Broadcast Communications. Now a millionaire, Bozo had taught him the power of television, which he used to once again bring magic into homes across America.

The first commercial for TV Magic Cards aired on November 18, 1969. It is a regular deck of cards with the exception that all cards can be shown as the same card. The idea for the Svengali deck was originated by magician Burling Hull in 1909. It had sold in magic shops for decades, and Brodien himself became familiar with the deck while working at the Treasure Chest. Some say that Brodien was "lucky" to hit on an idea that was not originally his own that sold over seventeen million decks. But it was not luck but thirty years of experience that went into the entire package. Harkening back to his carnie barker days at Riverview, Brodien made up a classic pitch. Ned Locke, aka Ringmaster Ned, did the voice-over for the first commercial:

Marshall Brodien's TV Magic Cards were a nostalgic favorite of the baby boomer generation. *Photo by author.*

"Even if you are all thumbs, you can do fantastic things with TV Magic Cards, the foolproof deck that works amazing card tricks all by itself."

Then there was the use of television, as his years working on *Bozo* gave Brodien an insight into just how powerful this "new" medium was. After its run on WGN, spots for TV Magic Cards, now read by Brodien ("Hi, I'm magician Marshall Brodien. Magic tricks are easy once you know the secret."), began running nationwide during such popular shows as *Get Smart* and *The Dick Van Dyke Show*. Soon, orders were coming in faster than they could print up the decks. One company said that if they wanted more decks, the price would go higher. Besides performing magic, magicians are foremost individual entrepreneurs. Brodien knew that he was being held over a barrel, and he turned to a man who seemed to have helped almost every magician in Chicago at one time or another: Jay Marshall. Marshall suggested Stancraft, a company that regularly printed magic cards. Brodien, Marshall and Rick Carey went into a meeting. They were not yet an official business and had only $8,000 in the bank. But the two Chicago greats worked their magic. Soon, Stancraft was printing an order for forty thousand decks. The rest is magic, television and Chicago nostalgia history.

Throughout the decades, Marshall continued to perform magic throughout Chicago and around the nation. Currently, he is retired and living in suburban Chicago in a large house—some might say a mansion. It was financed, primarily, by the tremendous sale of TV Magic Cards. Perhaps it is only fitting that a great magician should live in a "house of cards."

CHAPTER 10

MAGIGALS

FRANCES IRELAND

It is a stereotyped image ingrained in our psyche: While a male magician waves his wand, uncovers objects with a handkerchief or saws someone in half, a young woman, usually dressed in high heels, leggy black nylons and a half-tuxedo, stands next to him smiling, handing him props or climbing into the "saw box." At the end of the show, the magician extends his hand toward her while she bows and quickly scurries off the stage, picking up props as she goes. The assistant almost always knows the secret to each trick. Oftentimes she even helped to devise and implement it. So why isn't she standing over the box instead of inside it?

The answers as to why there have been so few female magicians, even with a changing society, are many. One answer lies in the roots of America and its founders. The performance of "magic" is still frowned upon by many communities. Four hundred years ago, it was even more pronounced. In 1692 in Salem, Massachusetts, twenty people were executed for practicing "witchcraft." Out of these, thirteen were women or girls, some who had not even reached their teens. The girls' crimes consisted mainly of hearing voices, screams and dancing in the woods. Despite the popularity and beauty of stars like Alyssa Milano in the television series *Charmed*, most girls still do not want to be called a "witch." It is no wonder that, over four hundred years later, many young women still shy away from expressing what might be a curiosity in magic. That, plus other social barriers such as females traveling "alone" on the road, the need to care for children and working in a male-dominated industry, still pervade even today. But there have been a few very notable exceptions to this pattern. Perhaps the most outstanding of these have very deep, if not lifetime, ties to the city of Chicago.

The first female magician to achieve wide international success was Adelaide. The wife of Alexander Herrmann, she traveled the world performing great feats of magic both before and after his death. History will also note that in his first years, Bess Houdini stood side by side with her husband, Harry, performing many of his tricks as well. After Harry Houdini's death, she performed in vaudeville, as her act included freezing a man in ice. While performing, Bess Houdini took even greater notice of the few female magicians on stage. In an effort to encourage more female magicians, Bess started the organization Magigals in 1938. Like the Society of American Magicians, which her husband had helped found, it was to provide a meeting place and forum for female magicians. Before the organization was founded, however, she turned to one magician in Chicago and chose her to be Magigals' co-founder. That woman was the co-owner of Ireland's Magic, Chicago's own Frances Ireland.

Ireland was born Frances Ahrens on Halsted Street in Chicago in 1910. One of eight children, she was from a working-class family and started work right out of high school. Some of the jobs she took included selling sheet music, working as a secretary and eventually authoring her first of many books and pamphlets, this one on how to raise mushrooms. The book came with a small mushroom growing kit that included a thermometer, fertilizer and seeds. The company made a small fortune but also received hundreds of complaints about how no mushrooms grew but their basements smelled like manure. Soon, the federal government cracked down on the operation. Ireland was out of a job, but she had learned something about the power of pamphlets and mail-order operations.

Located just below her old office was a shop called Miller's Magic Shop. Another, Arthur Felsman Magic, which boasted a six-foot statue of the devil, was located in the same series of shops. The third was run by a former carnival magician named Laurie Ireland. A bit of a drinker, he found it easier to hire the eager young unemployed secretary to type up his books. Within a short time, the two had produced Ideal Handkerchief Manipulation, Ireland's New Card and Coin Manipulation and magic tricks including a forest's dream and the multiplying golf balls. Soon, Ireland's Magic was born.

Laurie Ireland was known as a great magician, wit and man about town. Yet his skills did not include writing and typing. After she married Laurie

Frances Ireland and Jay Marshall take a break from Magic, Inc. and highlight their magical marriage. *Courtesy Sandy and Susan Marshall Collection.*

in 1940, Frances Ireland began producing books, pamphlets and magazine articles on or about magic. Ireland also began *Magicals Magazine*. She wrote a regular column called "Around Chicago" for *Linking Ring Magazine*. She wrote fifteen books, including *You Don't Have to Be Crazy* (1946), *With Frances in Magicland* (1952), *Kid Stuff* (six volumes, 1954–75), *How to Sell by Magic* (1958) and *The Sponge Book* (1960).

Although a talented magician and performer, Ireland was a small woman who was required to wear thick bifocal glasses and did not have the outgoing, flashy personality required to dominate the stage. Because of this, as well as cultural and social barriers, Ireland spent most of her career writing about magic, designing magic tricks and running Ireland's Magic Store and later Magic, Inc. When she did appear on stage, it was often performing magic for children or small audiences. Ireland was also a pioneer on the new medium of television. For more than five years, Frances appeared every Sunday in the *Funny Paper Party*, a program on WGN-TV featuring *Chicago Tribune* publisher Colonel Robert McCormick.

As stated in the Magic, Inc. section, Ms. Ireland married Jay Marshall in 1954. Marshall traveled often, performing around the world. Although she generally stayed in Chicago to oversee Magic, Inc., Ireland attended hundreds of magicians' conventions and gatherings.

When health issues forced her to retire from managing Magic, Inc., Frances's loss was quickly and deeply felt. Although a changing economy and neighborhood added to the complications, Jay Marshall made up for her loss by regularly writing checks to cover the shop's losses. Mrs. Marshall died of complications from congestive heart failure.

"Frances Marshall came from nothing and ended up being influential not only as one of the first female magicians but also for running Magic, Inc. for over half a century," Eugene Burger says. "She was brilliant, funny and clever and wrote many terrific articles and books on magic, including *With Frances in Magicland*, which I still remember today."

CHAPTER 11

CELESTE EVANS

BREAKING MORE BARRIERS

Celeste Evans walks out onto the stage. Standing in the arc of the spotlight, her shimmering gown, dark hair and green eyes give her the appearance of a movie star. As she stands on the platform, she performs a few simple tricks—small coins and other objects appear and disappear, cards change suits. But then, seemingly out of thin air, a white dove sits on her bare shoulder. Then, another one flutters its gentle wings in the spotlight. Where did they come from? They couldn't have been up her sleeve, as she is wearing a sleeveless gown. What is her secret? How can a woman do this trick?

With her poise, confidence, dark hair and shimmering gowns, Celeste Evans brought a touch of Hollywood glamour to Chicago's magic scene for over twenty-five years. Even her press photos were highlighted with the caption "The Beauty of Magic."

Yet as much as her beauty and poise were a help to her image, Evans spent much of her career silencing the few critics who could not believe that a woman or "girl" could become a top-flight magician. A native of White Rock, British Columbia, Canada, Evans grew up two miles north of the American border.

"We lived near the ocean," Evans says as she sits poolside in her home in St. Petersburg, Florida. "One day I went down to the beach and I saw two magicians, they were just teenagers, doing the magic trick of 'throwing' knots into silk. I asked them to teach me how to do it, and they said, 'You're a girl, and girls can't do magic.' Right then and there I told myself I was going to learn magic and become famous, even if it took me ten years."

Because she was a girl, Evans often practiced in secret in the bedroom of her farmhouse loft. In high school in Vancouver, she performed at a few parties and visited the local magic shops whenever she had the chance. But like most "good girls" of her time, she went on to secretarial school and became a secretary and stenographer at an accountant's office.

"I wasn't happy sitting at a desk all day doing numbers," Evans says. "I frequented a local magic shop run by a man named John Kirby. I told him I was interested in learning sleight of hand, and he told me for two dollars a lesson he could teach me. Two dollars was a lot of money in the early 1950s; I think I was making ninety dollars a month. But the lessons took hold fast, and after a while I told myself, 'Hey, I can do this.'"

Like many great magicians, Evans honed her craft on the carnival circuit. She traveled by canvas-backed truck across the dusty highway and snowcapped mountains with fire eaters, midgets and sword swallowers, with rides and animals not far behind. But her skill and beauty were quickly noticed in 1952 by a scout who saw her as the perfect person to entertain Commonwealth troops in Korea for the Canadian Legion. She was soon noticed by American officials, and over the next decade, Evans rarely had a chance to unpack her suitcase. She hit the magic circuit in the United States, but as time went on, her travels became more exotic. She says:

> *I toured the world several times. In 1957, I went on a United Nations tour and did a wonderful show in the Gaza Strip in Israel. Then we went to the Belgian Congo. It was three days after the start of the civil war. Innocent people were being killed, including six nuns. Once we got there, our plane— we were always on small planes that I barely thought could make it—well this one did but when it got to the airport, the plane was held hostage by rebels for eight hours. Then we had to perform on the back of a truck, and we barely finished the show when they began shooting machine guns, and I remember the truck driving away while the guns were firing.*

A tour of Europe, including Greenland, Iceland, France, Spain, Denmark and Sweden, was much more peaceful, but soon the world of the exotic called Evans once more.

"I went on a cultural exchange sponsored by President John F. Kennedy," Evans says. "We toured with the Buddy Rich Band and went to places like Laos, Singapore, Hong Kong and Nepal. I remember a prince from one of the countries kept insisting on holding my doves, and one of them pooped all over him."

During this time, Evans also became a star of television, appearing at the Palace Theater and on the *Ed Sullivan Show*, the *Arthur Godfrey Show* and *To Tell the Truth*. Her appearance on *To Tell the Truth* was probably the most dramatic. It was the days of old black-and-white television. Three beautiful young women stood on stage, bound by straightjackets. Each one stated, "I am Celeste Evans, professional magician and escape artist." Each was peppered with questions, and while Evans was cool and confident, speaking in a low, almost sultry voice, all three panelists thought contestant number three, a burlesque dancer, was Evans. The *To Tell the Truth* moment came when the real Celeste Evans shook, squirmed and wriggled her way out of the straightjacket in nine seconds while the other two stood helplessly.

While she was in New York, however, the ugly specter of sexism and discrimination once again reared its ugly head.

> *I was in demand, working all over New York at places like the Palace, and the male magicians wondered how a woman could get so many jobs. In their minds, it could never be because I was a great magician who had practiced since I was nine. After all, I was a woman. So they started filthy rumors. They said that I got my jobs because I slept for them. The worst was one day a man came up to me and said, "Oh, I know how you got the job, a trick for a trick."*

Although she showed America she could escape from a straightjacket in nine seconds, Evans realized that the only way to escape this situation was to leave the Big Apple.

> *I came to Chicago in 1962. It was during the Golden Age of Magic, and there was work everywhere. The banquet circuit was in high fashion, and so were the conventions. Now, people just e-mail, but in those days, you had wonderful conventions where people would meet. Chicago was a rail and air hub, and it had McCormack Place, this wonderful, giant arena. So some days we'd be doubling and tripling. There was also the Playboy Club, which was at first in an old firetrap, but then it moved to the building* [the Palm Olive Building] *next to the Drake Hotel. We loved to work at the Blackstone Hotel, the Palmer House, the Hilton, then the smaller clubs and bars. There was magic everywhere.*

While in Chicago, Evans met and wed Harry Breyn, owner of Breyn Management, a theatrical agency. Evans also gave birth to and began raising two children, Evan and Evanna, who helps to manage her mom's career today. In this way, Evans blazed a trail not only as a performer but also as a working mom. Now married and settled, Evans began to experience not only the nightlife but also the entire culture and history of Chicago. One of these areas was the Chicago Stockyards. Located roughly between Halsted and Damen to the east and west and Thirty-seventh and Forty-seventh Street to the north and south, the Chicago Stockyards were a city unto themselves. The setting of Upton Sinclair's *The Jungle*, the Stockyards employed over twenty-five thousand people, slaughtered over two million animals and were responsible for as much as 85 percent of the meat consumed in the United States in a year. They had their own rail lines, which had over 130 miles of track and almost 50 miles of road.

"Things were booming economically back then, especially in Chicago," Evans says. "I remember we would work at the Stockyards or at the steel mills in Chicago and Gary. They all worked different shifts, so we would get out and get up on stage for the 6:00 a.m. shift and then do another one at 4:30 or 5:00, and finally the midnight shift."

Much of Chicago's activity during this era can be attributed to the economy as a whole, as America may well have been at its most prosperous, but some can also be credited to the management and stability of longtime Chicago mayor Richard J. Daley. Daley was also one of Evans's biggest fans. She recalls:

> *Mayor Daley was always calling on me to perform at parties for his children and grandchildren, as he had a summer house on the lake* [Lake Michigan] *in Michigan* [Grand Beach] *just above the Indiana border. I was also asked to perform at Democratic rallies and fundraisers that Mayor Daley held. But my fondest memory of Mayor Daley was at one show he was sitting in the front row—he always sat in the front row—and one of my doves flew up into the spotlight.* [giggle] *And since it was flat and shiny, the dove landed on top of his head. And he started yelling at me, "Take the bird off, take the bird off!"*

Evans also appeared regularly on Chicago television, including thirty-three appearances on *Bozo's Circus*. After her husband passed away in 1984, Evans also took over the operations of Breyn Management. After touring with magicians, clowns, carnivals, musicians and other entertainers for over forty years, Evans definitely knew the entertainment business. In 1998, she was inducted into the Society of American Magicians Hall of Fame. In 2003, she retired from the agency, and she only recently left Chicago for the warmer climates of Florida.

The magical beauty of Celeste Evans and her doves. *Courtesy Celeste Evans.*

While performing, however, Evans made her mark on the world of magic, most notably for her work with doves.

I had no pockets, no sleeves, and although I started off with one, by the end I had as many as eight to ten doves. I was also the first one to have the doves illuminated all in fluorescent colors; what a sight it was, them flying at me in the spotlight. I was the only magician to do the birds in black light. I went to the factory that made the strobe light colors, and they made up a special formula for me to paint on them. After that, I got one dozen bottles a year.

As a woman, Evans also brought a new perspective to magic. Like Frances Ireland, she thought of children and often performed for them, making sure that children and families were part of the magic scene. "A lot of the old-time male magicians had these costumes with dark mustaches and black goatees. They didn't know that when children came, it scared them."

Evans also broke ground for many females, shattering the old tradition of the woman in tights working as the magician's assistants. "I felt sorry for all those girls who not only had to stand on stage and clap and run little errands, but after the show they would iron the silks and do laundry," Evans says. "They all knew the secrets of the tricks and secrets of the illusions but never performed themselves. "

But history, it seems, has its rewards, and Evans is far from forgotten for her work changing the face from the goatee to the "beauty of magic." "I still get letters from women and girls from all over the country asking me how they can become magicians," Evans says. "Just the other day, I got a letter from a nine-year-old in South Carolina. Her father then wrote and wanted to fly me there to give her lessons."

As the sun shines in St. Petersburg, Florida, Evans gazes out at her pool and ponders. "Nine years old. That's the same age I saw those boys on the ocean and decided I wanted to be a magician—because they said I couldn't do it because I was a girl."

Chapter 12

Maritess Zurbano

Girlie Magic for the New Millennium

The great magicians of the past, including Blackstone and Thurston, practiced levitation and toured the country with magic shows that resembled rolling magical tent caravans. Magician Maritess Zurbano also performs levitations and tours nationally, but the similarities definitely end there.

A native of Chicago's Brighton Park neighborhood, Zurbano is a woman of Filipino descent who has studied to be an artist, worked as a dealer and card sharp in Las Vegas, written plays and toured the nation with her own magic show. Like Celeste Evans, whom she lists as one of her role models, and Frances Marshall, whom she saw many times while hanging around Magic, Inc., Zurbano had to overcome working as a female magician in a male world. Yet Zurbano also had to overcome barriers both inside and outside her culture as an Asian female.

"I was born at Mount Sinai Hospital and lived in Brighton Park until I was in third grade, when we moved to Willowbrook, Illinois, a new and mostly white area," Zurbano says. "I hated it. Classmates called me tsetse fly and jungle bunny—we were all so young, I don't think any of us really knew what that meant, but I had a feeling it was something they heard growing up."

Like many children, Zurbano was fascinated with magic stories and images of angels and other stories from her Catholic upbringing. But while most people just see these interests as a diversion of their youth, Zurbano followed up on it as she became a young woman. She says:

Maritess Zurbano has continued to break gender and cultural barriers with her magical talent and creativity. *Photo by Misa Martin.*

I looked up "magic" in the phone book, and there was Magic, Inc. I took private magic lessons from Bob Brown. He passed away just a few years ago. He taught me sleight of hand, and his kind and charming performance style is one of my biggest influences. This is also where I briefly met Frances Marshall. Due to her reputation and influence on the magic community, I believe this is why every single Chicago magician I've ever met has always treated me (and I'm sure any female magician) as an equal with respect and kindness. Jay [Marshall], *of course, was a legend, but at that time, I really didn't understand what a big deal he actually was. I thought he as a nice old man who wore cardigan sweaters and owned our little magic shop.*

Once out of high school, Zurbano received a scholarship to the School of the Art Institute in Chicago. Using an uncle who was also an artist as a role model, Zurbano began to study art, which was another outlet for her passions. After initially studying painting and drawing, she characteristically moved into more hands-on "male-dominated" mediums like sculpture, holography, welding and woodworking.

"By attending art school in the big city, it was my chance to escape the homogenized suburbs and insert myself into the worldly atmosphere of the Art Institute, which I have revered since my first school field trip as a child and recurring school trips every year," Zurbano says. "It was a great place for expression and experimentation."

Zurbano's art skills also allowed her to continue to study magic. At the time, Brown was in the process of publishing a book, *Bob's Busking Balloons*. Zurbano says:

> *I was studying photography in college, so he asked me to do the photo illustrations in exchange for $200 in magic books and supplies. I remember one day me, Bob and Jay spent a sunny afternoon in the park. Bob busked, and I took photos. When I told Jay to get out of the way in one shot, he looked surprised, as if he has never been asked not to be in a photo. We had so much fun that I felt that the magic world was a special beautiful community and wanted to be a permanent resident.*

Although she was taught hands-on by older master magicians in Chicago, Zurbano's imagination and drive were also influenced by the "superstar" national magicians who often appeared on television or had shows in large theaters or posh hotels.

> *I was strongly influenced by Copperfield and Lance Burton, mainly because they were both super cute in their youth. I was way too young to really understand what Copperfield was doing, but I enjoyed that he had black eyes and brown hair, like me. He was the closest thing to being Filipino next to Desi Arnaz on TV. Lance looks really hot topless, and back in the 1990s, I was struck by the fact that when he was topless, he was actually catering to the women in the audience, as opposed to most magic shows which only appeal to the straight male fantasy. Also, Lance is a highly skilled magician and has been nothing but generous and kind to me and my family when we went to see his shows in Vegas. I admire my mentor, Gary Darwin, of course, for his amazing skill at sleight of hand and our mutual obsession with art making and magic culture. I also admire Kevin James for his wonderful inventiveness. I'm a big fan of Marco Tempest for his groundbreaking use of technology with magic and not making it*

look like the technology was actually behind the secret of the magic effect. My favorite magician, of course, is my other mentor, Paula Paul, who is a real-life shaman and sorceress. Her street-smart cosmopolitan nature is really what gave me hope that women could really own magic, could really become their own definition of magic, rather than a man's imaginings of how a woman could possibly wield power.

After her stint in art school, Zurbano moved to Las Vegas, where she worked as a blackjack dealer. There, she became even more adept at manipulating cards, a key skill in the tool chest of any magician. She then got a job at a Las Vegas magic shop and used her guile to obtain her first paid magic job.

I happened to answer the phone when they asked for a magician. At that point, I was living in Vegas for about a year. I saw so many incompetent people getting paid to do magic, I thought well, if they could do it, so can I. After that, with every magic show came more confidence and skill, and that's when I started contacting Las Vegas agents. There was a lot of work for local magicians in the 1990s. It was when there was a lot of construction of new casinos and Vegas was getting a marketing makeover as a meeting destination.

From there, Zurbano took the enormous step of transforming herself from a popular local act to a national figure. Just as her influence, Frances Ireland, invented Magigals, Zurbano created her own one-woman magical show stressing her gender—titled *Girliemagic*. Combining her skills in art and artistic production, magic and writing for theater, Zurbano took her show to New York. While growing up in Chicago and working the casinos in Las Vegas gave Zurbano an inner toughness, she had yet to experience the shark tank known as the Big Apple.

I learned a lot about New York's alternative theater scene from that experience; mainly, it is essential that every playwright become a member of the Dramatists Guild. The DG lawyer protected me when a couple of people attempted to bully and claim intellectual property over my magic show/play creation. The lesson for all artists is to stand your ground, accept that part of being a professional artist means that you must familiarize yourself with business and legal issues, no matter how much you loathe it, because it can directly affect your art making. And don't be afraid to obtain advice from mentors and professional arts organizations.

Like many of the great magicians of vaudeville, Zurbano then took "magic stories" on the road nationally. "I pretty much traveled with a bunch of suitcases and boxes, and my assistants/staff/technical crew/producers were in the destination city," says Zurbano, who is also penning her own memoir, *Misdirection*, about becoming a female performer in a male-dominated field. "We rehearsed in the destination city for between a week and a month, depending on the complexity of the show. I received a lot of volunteer hours from dozens of very talented people who did it simply because they believed in me and my magic vision, which was so wonderful."

Over the years, Zurbano has returned several times to Chicago, where she performed at Magic Chicago with her friend Benjamin Barnes, as well as alumni shows at the Art Institute and benefits for Asian-American organizations.

"I'll probably be in Chicago on a yearly basis, as I'm focusing on performing my new stage hypnosis show at colleges around the country," Zurbano says. "I also like visiting Chicago because I have a million cousins and some close friends who still live there."

CHAPTER 13

BIZARRE MAGIC CHICAGO

For much of the early twentieth century, images of floating skulls, mist, ghosts, devils and demons dancing around a cauldron while a master magician waved his wand graced the posters of master magicians from Kellar to Blackstone Sr. During this era, magic was performed to a largely unsophisticated population. Performances of magic often began with long-winded speeches about conjuring mystic powers and supernatural forces working to change what "we" see, hear and feel.

As time went on, the rise of nightclub magic and the onset of radio, television variety shows and the sophisticated urban culture changed this. Magic was now a show, and great magicians became famous for accompanying their performances with jokes, humorous stories and comic banter. Yet as the 1970s arrived, a group of magicians, based largely in Chicago, also brought magic back to its American roots. In doing so, they invented *Bizarre Magic*.

"In the early 1970s, there was a backlash against magic and how it was being performed at that time," Neil Tobin, president of the Chicago Chapter of the Society of American Magicians, says.

Magic had become very much in the style of a man in a tuxedo, a series of poof, poofs and a joke or two, kind of like the characters in the movie The Incredible Burt Wonderstone. *In many areas, magic had become just entertainment, reduced to visuals. But magic can be intensely powerful. A group of people set out to change this, but when one guy, Tony Andruzzi,*

Chicagoan Eugene Burger, known as one of the most accomplished magicians in America, also helped to pioneer *Bizarre Magic* in Chicago. *Photo by Richard Faverty/ Beckett Studios.*

began publishing the magazine The New Invocation, *which was printed on the presses in the back of Magic, Inc., the movement found a leader.*

Tony Andruzzi was born Timothy McGuire in Cheyenne, Wyoming, in 1925. At age one, he was adopted by Charles and Gertrude Palmer and named Thomas Palmer. As a young man, he became a traveling magician, gaining a name for himself as Thomas S. Palmer. He published several books on magic, including *The Flea Circus Act* and *Modern Illusions.*

During the late 1960s, he moved to Chicago. His act as Palmer already featured "bizarre" elements such as the Satan's seat illusion, which he invented in 1959. His second wife, Gloria Jacobson, was also an artist who performed under the name Vampira. But the move to Chicago seemed to spark his creative juices. Part of it may have been the hippie culture that was blossoming around him on Chicago's North Side and lakefront neighborhoods. Business cards from the era listed his address as 420 West Melrose. Nearby areas like Wells Street near Old Town and later Clark Street near Diversey Parkway were filled with head shops, strolling guitar players, Hare Krishnas and young people in fringe, bell-bottoms and mini-skirts. In 1970, he legally changed his name to Antonio C. Andruzzi.

With a new persona, Andruzzi went on to lecture, publish and host events like "The Invocational." Soon, he was joined by other magicians including Jeff McBride, Tony "Doc" Shields, Eugene Burger and, later, Neil Tobin.

Bizarre Magic brought back other older forms of magic that were once used by magicians at the turn of the twentieth century. These included Spiritualism and showing the audience that there was a magical world far beyond the one that is present in the room. The first and easiest way to change the atmosphere of the room and bring in another realm was through setting the scene, or storytelling. The story, in turn, creates an atmosphere where the audience feels closer.

"Magic is storytelling," Tobin says. "As a performing art, it elicits deep emotions based on our desire to touch what is unknown—to give the audience a sense of wonder."

Eugene Burger, a friend, follower and champion of Andruzzi and *Bizarre Magic*, explained how he uses storytelling to elicit the imaginations of the audience and begin to take them into a more magical realm.

"I might begin by making the cards themselves important," Burger told the British Magic Circle. "If I just take a deck of cards out of my pocket and toss it onto the table and start, that's one way to go about it. But what if I take the pack out of my pocket, hold it up, look at it and say something like, 'I've always been fascinated with playing cards, fortunes have been won or lost, loves have come and gone, on the turn of a single card.'"

Burger, who also has degrees in philosophy and divinity from Yale University and has taught university courses in comparative religion and philosophy, explains the reasoning behind such an introduction. "Now, I'm giving the deck of cards themselves a mythology," Burger says. "In the process, I'm trying to elevate what I'm doing."

Besides storytelling, *Bizarre Magic* also used stage props like candles, dark curtains and eerie music to set the scene. At times, Andruzzi entered the room accompanied by bagpipes.

Visually, Andruzzi turned the clock back to the days of European magicians like Robert Houdin and Alexander Herrmann by appearing with dyed black hair and a dark goatee and speaking to the audience in a low, mysterious voice. His repertoire included plunging a needle into his arm and pushing it deeper and deeper without drawing one drop of blood, turning a skeleton key without touching it and making a rock move as if it was breathing.

Andruzzi's publications included *Modern Illusion*, *The Tie Patch* and *Vampira*, all published under the name Tom Palmer by Magic, Inc. As Tony Andruzzi, he published *Complete Invocation* volumes I, II and III. He was also featured in Eugene Burger's 1990 video, *Eugene Goes Bizarre*.

Andruzzi died in Chicago's Northwestern Hospital on December 22, 1991. Yet *Bizarre Magic* and some of its elements are now included in the acts of magicians like Eugene Burger, who told *Genii Magazine*:

> *Tony's aim, I think, was to pull the rug from under our concept of reality, to shake us up, to disturb us. Tony gave all of us permission to take our magic into new and different directions, to walk down different paths. This was extremely important for us and, I think, for magic. As a friend, I greatly miss Tony. He could cheerfully fix anything that I broke and he had a wonderfully devilish smile!*

Today, Neil Tobin also uses elements of *Bizarre Magic* in his long-running Chicago show, *Supernatural Chicago*. In 2010, he also co-authored the book *Unspeakable Acts: Three Lives and Countless Legends of Tom Palmer, Tony Andruzzi and Masklyn ye Mage*.

CHAPTER 14

WALTER E. KING, AKA "SPELLBINDER"

REGAL MAGIC

Walter E. King has opened for such stars as Whitney Houston, Bill Cosby, the Temptations and James Brown. He has also performed at legendary venues like the Mirage in Las Vegas, the Sands and one of the bastions for African American culture in Chicago, the Regal Theater.

In his younger days, King would arrive at a performance driving a gray 1962 Cadillac hearse. As he emerged from the macabre automobile, he would then turn on a fog machine that he had in the vehicle. Often dressed in sequins and accompanied by beautiful assistants, King had the crowd in the palm of his hand before he even entered the venue, earning his moniker "Spellbinder." Now, he amazes audiences with both the old version of the broomstick levitation and a new version featuring light sabers that flash and glow like meteors on the stage. But perhaps his most noted effect is his take on the "lady in the box." King puts a young woman in a large box with a smaller box on top. King opens the large box, and you see the woman's torso. Then, he opens a smaller, separate compartment on top. There is the woman's face. Suddenly, King twirls the box, and the woman's head rotates 360 degrees, all to the music of Sam Cooke's "Twisting the Night Away." This penchant for drama and show business was learned during decades of performing magic as well as acting in major motion pictures. But like many Chicagoland magicians and children of his era, his first exposure to magic came via one of the classic segments from the Golden Era of Chicago Television.

Walter E. King, aka Spellbinder, has performed with the likes of Bill Cosby, Whitney Houston and James Brown. *Courtesy Walter E. King.*

"When I was seven, I saw something that amazed me and changed my life," King says. "I was watching *Garfield Goose and Friends*, and suddenly I saw a pair of hands on a black background—the Magic Hands. I watched as they did things like making a penny disappear inside of a metal box, the genie in the bottle rope trick. I was fascinated with how they did it, and it showed you just how the rubber meets the road."

From there, King expanded his knowledge of magic, traveling downtown to stores like the Treasure Chest to buy magic supplies, seeing David Copperfield perform and even looking into ventriloquism. He began doing small magic shows around the neighborhood and amazed students in grade school science class when he made a beaker of water disappear. But as he approached his impressionable teen years, peer pressure made him put a temporary end to his hobby.

"I grew up on the West Side in 'the hood' at Forty-seventh Street and Cicero Avenue," King says. "I was going around doing magic, but the brothers just weren't getting it, so I had to put the stuff down for a while.

While attending Chicago's Farragut High School, King, like many magicians of the modern era, took up theater. He was overjoyed when he landed a small role in the film *One in a Million, the Ron Leflore Story* and was set on a career in acting. After studying theater and graduating from Chicago's Columbia College, King got a few more acting roles in small and student films. While appearing in local theater, King's interest in magic once again became useful.

"I was doing a solo dance routine, and I saw something at a magic shop on Irving Park Road that would make a cane disappear. I used it in a show, and they loved it. Somebody asked me if I could do magic for ten minutes. I couldn't do magic for five minutes, but I said yes and kept on doing it. As long as it paid for itself, I kept on doing it, but soon magic starting paying me."

As an African American magician, King was something of an anomaly. He appeared on segments inside the community like the television show *The Ebony Jet Showcase* and doing shows for Soft Sheen Products. Then he hit the mainstream, as by 1984 he was performing at the Mirage and the Sands in Las Vegas and the Aerie Crown Theater in Chicago. Thus the "Spellbinder" was born. Soon, he was in demand all over the country and was hired as an opening act for people like Bill Cosby, Whitney Houston, Jennifer Hudson, the Temptations, James Brown at the African Heritage Festival in Chicago's Washington Park and many more.

"I got in with Jam productions, which produces a lot of concerts in the Chicago area," King says. "To be honest, a lot of these gigs are last-minute calls, when the venue, not the artist, decides they need a warm-up act or maybe somebody else didn't show up. But I enjoyed working with all of them. Being around such talent is something that I will always be grateful for."

Besides his talents, Spellbinder also attracted attention by incorporating the flashy show business angles he learned while he was working as an actor. "I drove to gigs in a 1962 Cadillac hearse," King says. "It freaked people out. I did it more for security than show. I needed something to carry my equipment in, as I had problems with people breaking in. I had a van, but a friend of mine who was a musician sold me the hearse because he said nobody would bother it. And he was right! So much that one day I was in a hurry to start the show and I left the keys hanging in the door—but nobody ever tried to take the car."

King arrived at venues accompanied by a fog machine that he kept in the back of his "ever secure" hearse and also enjoyed using other gags to attract attention, including one that harkens back to his childhood days. "I kept a hand between the seats of my car," King says. "When people were watching, I would levitate it toward the window and make it move, kind of like the 'Magic Hand' on *Garfield Goose*."

Between his unique act and show business skills, King is continually in demand, playing as many as forty shows a month. He has been featured as part of Magic Chicago four times and also works diligently for his church, as his latest venture is a gospel production entitled *War of the Spirits*.

"I got into magic as a hobby, hoping it would pay for itself," King says. "But for most of my life it has been paying me, and I am grateful for that and all of the wonderful opportunities that magic has given me in my life."

CHAPTER 15

SEAN MASTERSON

RESTORING THE EARLY DAYS OF MAGIC

Sean Masterson is standing on stage at Chicago's Witt Theater. Dressed in a long brown coat with tails, gray top hat, striped trousers, pointed collar shirt and scarf-like tie, he is the picture of a perfect gentleman, circa 1890. As the crowd files in on a warm spring afternoon, Masterson sets down a large satchel-like bag, like the ones vaudeville performers may have used or those from the cartoons on the carpetbaggers drawn after the Civil War. Billed as the "Magic Matinee," Masterson's shows specialize in depicting the world of magic, circa 1890s.

"Today I am going to take you back into another world," Masterson says. "A world back in the days of the great magicians, like Alexander Herrmann and his wife, Adelaide, who used to arrive in Chicago's Auditorium Hotel with a show that consisted of thirteen rail cars and ten men to set it up. Well," Masterson says, smiling, "my show will not be that extravagant, but I will still take you back to an era some call the Golden Age of Magic."

After performing a series of card tricks and coaxing flowers, red rubber balls and other objects to appear and reappear at will, Masterson is now ready to commence the major part of his show.

"We will need someone from the audience to assist us," he says. Wading up the aisle and into the audience, he points to a shy, petite brunette wearing a short summer dress.

"Have a seat," he says, pointing to the stage. "I have a book for you: *Macbeth*. Have you read it in high school?" The young woman laughs as he hands her the book.

Sean Masterson is bringing back the magic of vaudeville to audiences throughout Chicagoland. *Courtesy Sean Masterson.*

"What I want you to do is pick out a word. The play is thousands of words long, but I want you to pick out just one, any word in the text."

The young woman sits silently and then writes it down. Masterson then takes out a long scroll of paper. Unraveling it across the stage, the word "tiger" appears in bright red letters. The woman puts her hand over her mouth. Opening the sealed paper, the word she has picked is "tiger." The audience cheers as the young woman, blushing and looking for her boyfriend in the crowd, makes her way off the stage.

Masterson says from his North Side condominium:

> *In Chicago, the crowd that comes to magic shows is mostly one of theatergoers. They don't come out to see a magic show with lots of glitz and giant props and animals. That they can see in Las Vegas. What they want is something akin to the theater experience. They are intelligent people who want a story, they want to see, hear and come away almost like they had seen a play, learning something that has a meaning.*

Masterson did not arrive at this thesis overnight. Instead, it evolved over three decades of studying the great magicians, practicing his trade and performing throughout the United States and Europe at any type of venue that would draw a crowd. A native of Lombard, Illinois, Masterson's introduction to the world of magic came via the popular invention of Marshall Brodien. He says:

> *I started doing magic when I was seven, after I received a set of TV Magic Cards. After a while, I started doing shows in libraries and competing in contests, and when I was twelve, I was named as Junior Magician of the Year. I continued to read about Houdini and other well-known magicians. Then I saw a photo of Cardini, with his monocle, top hat, white gloves and thin mustache. I became fascinated with him and his history.*

In his early teens, he joined a junior magicians' club. Now able to venture into the city, Masterson took lessons, saw shows and bought props from Magic, Inc. In high school, he performed in many school productions, which led to his enrolling at Illinois State University to study theater.

"I always knew that I wanted to be a performer," Masterson says, "and after college, I moved to San Francisco, where I began performing in nightclubs."

Masterson continued to develop his stage craft through working and performing on cruise ships and various shows ranging from Canada to

California to Key West, Florida. Eventually, he felt it was time to return to Chicago, where he performed close-up magic at bars and restaurants like Toppo Giggio and other North Side locations. After brushing up on his skills, Masterson decided to test his skills as a headliner.

"I did my first show at the Shattered Globe Theater, on Halsted near the old Steppenwolf," Masterson says. "It was a self-produced show where I handed out posters, sold tickets and did all other promotions."

From there he moved to Sheffield's, a theater near Wellington and Sheffield Streets, not far from Wrigley Field. During this production, he continued to develop his theme of combining magic, theater and history.

"The show was called *Magic Tales*, and it got rave reviews," Masterson says. "Bill Kurtis, of CBS/WBBM TV, became a fan and booster. Jay Marshall, who I met in 1990, also started coming to my shows. After that he came to all of my shows, and afterward he would talk to me and give me some kind of encouragement or advice. Eugene Burger also attended my shows."

In 2002, he produced *Conjuring Time* at the Live Bait Theater and performed at the Actors Gymnasium as well. Always fascinated with magic and vaudeville, Masterson finally began to seriously combine the two themes in 2006. The idea came to fruition at Chicago's Music Box Theatre. Chicago's oldest full-time theater, it was built in 1929 and was the first theater in Chicago specifically built and designed for sound pictures. Ironically, it was the coming of the talkie that sounded the first death knell for vaudeville, but the roots of Masterson's show harkened back to the days of silent film, complete with a restored pipe organ.

"I performed with the organ at 11:00 a.m.," Masterson says. "At that time, they were showing Laurel and Hardy films, mostly for children, and it was obvious that they were trying to get people in the theater at an off hour. So I went to the manager with what I thought was a win-win situation. I guaranteed them a certain amount at the gate and did all the publicity and even hired the organist, Kim Clark, to come in." Luckily, the show was a success, as Masterson not only met but often exceeded his "guarantee" of one hundred people per show.

Afterward, he continued to develop the link between his show and performances and the master magicians of vaudeville. More and more, he began sporting the long tails, top hat and triangular collared shirts of the era. He also began performing at older venues, like the Morse Theater in Rogers Park, a former vaudeville house and silent film venue, as well as the Driehaus Museum. The Gilded Age home of Chicago banker Samuel Mayo Nickerson, it was turned into a museum by Chicago philanthropist

Masterson united the tradition of magic with Chicago's oldest movie theater, the Music Box. *Courtesy Sean Masterson.*

Richard H. Driehaus in 2003. Filled with ornately carved wooden staircases and trim, chandeliers and decorative stained glass by Louis Comfort Tiffany, artwork and plaster and terra-cotta pillars, it would have been a fitting spot for Alexander Herrmann.

"Many of the great magical tricks and theories are so much a passing on or interface with something that was invented or performed long ago, so it is not only interesting but an essential part of our craft to study the magicians of the past," Masterson says. In doing so, Masterson concludes his show with homage to Robert Herrmann. As he speaks to the audience, a white-gloved hand appears in a frame. Slowly, the hand moves, floating, dancing and drifting while the audience sits, mouths agape. This act of performing, amazement and the indescribable effect of actually seeing magic and magicians live is what Sean Masterson and the art of magic are all about. He says:

> *If you notice, Broadway plays and theater in general have been gaining in popularity. People are paying high prices, often more than $200 a ticket, to see a show that will run for more than a year, sometimes several years. That is because people want a connection, they want a live experience. Music, film, books have all been downloaded and digitized so you can access it on your computer. Theater, and live magic in theater, is one thing that you cannot digitize.*

CHAPTER 16

MAGIC CHICAGO

EVERY FIRST WEDNESDAY OF THE MONTH

B ill Cook is standing on stage next to a large CD player boom box holding a shiny compact disc. He waves his hands and throws it in the air. Yet as the disc rises, the single CD somehow multiplies itself until Cook is surrounded by compact discs floating in the air. They all fall to the ground accompanied by a wave of applause from the audience. Cook goes backstage to get a broom to sweep up the discs, but now the CDs have melded to the floor. Scratching his head, Cook exits stage right. From stage left.

Magic Chicago is a monthly magic and variety show that takes place the first Wednesday of every month at Stage 773 at 1225 West Belmont in Chicago. Like so many events and movements in the world of Chicago magic, the original fingerprints on this document also come from Eugene Burger.

"The idea started when Eugene Burger had a handful of students who made a core group of magicians," Benjamin Barnes, one of the show's stars and producers, says. "The three core members were myself, Robert Charles and Patrick Thomas Murphy, who were all practicing magicians who had no place to perform."

In July 2005, however, Magic Chicago found its first home at the Summerdale Community Church at Foster and Ashland. The first three shows were by invitation only, but word soon spread. The show grew so quickly that it ran out of room at the church, and in February 2006, it moved to the City Lit Theater. It soon attracted major magicians, including Max Maven, Jeff McBride and Tina Lenert, as well as Eugene Burger, Sean Masterson and Dennis Watkins. The genre was mostly close-up magic, but

MAGIC CHICAGO

CHICAGO'S PREMIER SHOWCASE FOR MAGIC, MYSTERY AND WONDER

Above: Magic Chicago is helping to bring the Golden Age of Magic back to Chicago. *Courtesy Magic Chicago.*

Left: Benjamin Barnes helped to start Magic Chicago along with the omnipresent Eugene Burger. *Photo by Johnny Knight.*

soon the show expanded to include an even greater variety of entertainers. A recent show included "Vicious and Delicious," two acrobat/contortionists from San Francisco. During one part of the show, Etienne McGinley, aka Vicious, balances on a bowling ball that is set on top of a four- by six-inch piece of wood that is, in turn, set atop a small table. A short time later, his partner, Leah Orleans, aka Delicious, stands on top of McGinley's feet while he is doing a handstand. Part magic, part old-time vaudeville, Magic Chicago is almost like a modern version of the *Ed Sullivan Show*.

"It became sort of an open mic, as we had musicians, jugglers, comedians, acrobats, jugglers who give the show a bit of variety for the audience," Barnes says.

The mainstay performers have been magicians Robert Charles, who is a member of London's Magic Circle, and Barnes. A native of Chicago's South Side Jeffrey Manor neighborhood, Barnes grew up in show business.

"My father was the fire marshal at the Regal Theater," Barnes says of the South Side landmark where legendary performers ranging from Duke Ellington to the Jackson Five, Miles Davis, James Brown, the Temptations, Bill Cosby and so many others performed. "When I was a kid, they had a lot of great singers and bands, but they also had magicians, and it was his job to keep the magicians from burning the place down."

As a teenager, Barnes was mesmerized by performers like Top Hat and Walter King Jr., aka Spellbinder. While attending St. Francis De Sales High School in Chicago, Barnes spent his evenings watching magicians like Spellbinder. It was at this time that Barnes got the "magic bug." It struck on and off through high school, but like Celeste Evans, Watkins, Tobin and so many others, the thought of working nine-to-five for the rest of his life "shocked" him into the world of magic. Soon he became a student of Burger's, which led to performances at the Magic Castle in Los Angeles, as well as for corporate clients including Mc Donald's, Pepsi and the Chicago Bulls. But his favorite performance spot and magical "home" will always be Magic Chicago.

"It is a place where the audience can see some of the greatest established magicians, as well as young performers breaking in," Barnes says. "We also have contortionists, jugglers and comedians—there is something unique every month, and it is live, usually unrehearsed and something you cannot see on television."

CHAPTER 17

NEIL TOBIN AND SUPERNATURAL CHICAGO

MAGIC AND CHICAGO HAUNTINGS

Made out of thick brown limestone and featuring two castle-like turrets, columns and gargoyles, Castle Chicago, formerly Excalibur, is one of the oldest standing buildings in Chicago today. It is also one of the most haunted. So it comes as no surprise that magician, psychic and self-described necromancer Neil Tobin has made it the home of his hit show, *Supernatural Chicago*. The show has been praised by the *Chicago Reader*, *Red Eye*, the *Chicago Tribune*, A&E's *Sightings*, WGN TV, *Centerstage Chicago* and the *Chicago Sun-Times*. But perhaps the greatest praise comes from one's peers, and fellow magician Eugene Burger wrote in *Genii Magazine*, "Tobin presents a delightful evening of ghost stories, each with a Chicago connection [in *Supernatural Chicago*]…All in all, a most enjoyable evening."

The show opened on Friday the thirteenth, 2004, and has been entertaining and shocking audiences ever since.

"Magic, as a performing art, elicits a very deep instinct we have that is based on our desire to touch what is unknown and give us an explanation and understanding," Tobin says.

A native of Chicago's northern suburbs who attended Niles West High School, Tobin describes himself in his show as a necromancer. "The term is derived from the Greek word *necro*, which means dead," Tobin says. "A necromancer is one who can speak with the departed to forecast the future in a continuation of a whole variety of magic and psychic gifts."

Tobin first felt that he had these gifts as a child, experiencing feelings of intuition and communication with others involving thoughts and ideas that

Supernatural Chicago combines magic and tales of Chicago's legendary ghosts in a building that many say is among the most haunted in Chicago. *Courtesy Neil Tobin.*

were transmitted in a non-verbal manner, often with those he was not in direct contact with.

"We all have those times when we are thinking about a friend or relative that we have not seen or heard from in a long time, and suddenly the phone rings and it is them," Tobin says. "When I tried to talk about these experiences to adults, I was considered on the fringe, but nevertheless I went to the library and started reading every book about magic, magic history, ghosts and haunting that I could."

Tobin began performing magic at small shows and parties in high school, but his attention turned to English and drama at Northern Illinois University. Tobin went on to law school for one year. But a visit to Hollywood's Magic Castle rekindled his interest in magic. Tobin first gained major attention citywide for the reenactment of the Houdini séance. As Houdini was president of the Chicago Assembly of Society of American Magicians, Tobin believed that Chicago would be a perfect place to contact the spirit of the great Houdini.

"After all, Houdini was the first president of SAM, and Chicago was a major magic and entertainment hub from the days of vaudeville, as all you had to do was step off the train. That may be one reason why Houdini himself came here to organize the Chicago Chapter of SAM, which was the third chapter."

The event draws from elements of magic, psychic abilities and historic recreation of a Victorian séance. Now held annually on October 31, the night of Houdini's death, Tobin's show, which is held at the Castle, formerly Excalibur at 632 North Dearborn, has become one Chicago's most sought-after tickets to celebrate the Halloween season.

"SAM was looking for a historic place to hold the séance, and they [the Castle] not only said yes, but the event and the idea went over so well that we talked about having a show with the idea of Spiritualism there year round," Tobin says.

Spiritualism, magic and ghosts, it seemed, all fit well at Excalibur/the Castle. Originally built in 1892, the building was the first home of the Chicago Historical Society. Before that time, the site was the private residence of early Chicago settler John La Lime. Legend has it that he was murdered by John Kinzie, who is recognized as one of the city's founding fathers, over a land dispute. The building also served as a bar, hotel and private residence before it was made into a public nightclub, the Limelight, and then renamed Excalibur in 1989 and the Castle in 2012.

"Employees there talk about bottles being rolled from shelves, personages like a [man] nattily dressed in the fashion of the last century, standing at the bar on the second floor, or a woman in a red and white dress, or a little girl

Neil Tobin conjures magic, ghosts and excitement at his weekly performance. *Photo by Jonathan Cohon.*

running around," Tobin says. "So in this way, the club is the perfect place in which to hold the [*Supernatural Chicago*] event."

Supernatural Chicago also brings other Chicago ghost stories and hauntings, such as Resurrection Mary, the "Devil Baby" of Hull House and the Eastland Disaster, all taken from "an entire city built on the site of its own cremation." Tobin combines this with magic sleight of hand such as bending and melting coins in people's hands, sending cards flying through the room and starting spontaneous flames. He also stuns audiences with his mind-bending magic of reading dates, names and other events that the show's attendees have locked deep inside their consciousness.

"We now live in an age where technology gives us everything, especially on the computer," Tobin says. "We have more news, more TV shows, more movies, but what we don't understand is that people are craving for something that these technologies do not give. That," Tobin says, "is the childish feeling of mystery, amazement and wonder at something we may or may not see but cannot understand."

CHAPTER 18

DENNIS WATKINS

REVIVING HOUDINI AND MAGIC AT THE PALMER HOUSE

Dennis Watkins is standing in a black tunic-style bathing suit, circa 1920s. Next to him is a Plexiglas tank filled with water. Known as the Chinese water torture cell, it represents one of Harry Houdini's greatest and most dangerous escapes. Holding a pair of goggles in one hand, Watkins steps forward. An assistant then walks out with four sets of foot stocks. A medieval device used for punishment, they consist of two long boards with holes cut in the center. The two boards are separated, and the bottoms of Watkins's legs are placed inside. An assistant calls out to the audience at Chicago's House Theater: "We need two people to inspect and close the locks."

Two people step forward, almost reluctantly, wondering if they will be part of a man's doom. The two boards are brought back together, the holes tight around the ankles so his feet and legs are totally immobile. After the audience members inspect them, the devices are locked. His feet now enclosed in four heavy stocks, a pulley raises Watkins feet first, so he now hangs upside down over the tank. Watkins is now lowered inside, his feet immobile, upside down in a tank not much larger than a phone booth. Then, a lid is placed over it. On top of the lid, four heavy chains are wrapped around the "phone booth." The chains are then locked with thick padlocks. A voice booms over the theater's speakers. A large clock is brought out, and the red second hand begins sweeping. During the time Watkins was lowered and the padlocks secured, more than twenty precious seconds have already ticked off.

Dennis Watkins, star of
Death and Harry Houdini,
brings forth fire, water
and magic with his
weekly show at Chicago's
Palmer House Hotel.
Courtesy Dennis Watkins.

"Houdini will now attempt to escape from the cell, but he has merely three minutes in which to do it. In case he cannot," the assistant continues, "we have a man ready with a sledgehammer to break the glass."

What the audience does not know, however, is that the Plexiglas is actually too thick to be broken by a sledgehammer. Now Watkins has only two and a half minutes to escape. As he hangs there holding his breath literally for dear life, some in the audience may wonder, "How did he get here? Why does he do this?"

Watkins says from his home on Chicago's North Side:

> As a child, my grandfather ran a magic shop called Douglas Magicland. He hired great magicians like Mark Wilson and a man who called himself Willard the Wizard. Actually, there were four Willard the Wizards, as the act was passed down through the generations, but they had a tent show that traveled through the Southwest, and he also spent a lot of time at my

grandfather's store. So it is easy to see how I became hooked, and I have basically been doing magic since I was seven.

Like many modern-era magicians, Watkins received training in theater, his from Southern Methodist University. In 2001, he moved to Chicago, where he met a group of actors who began the House Theater. Today, the House Theater has its own space at the Chopin Theater, 1543 West Division Street. In 2001, however, the struggling company was looking for an identity and a home. Watkins had to look no further than his childhood in magic and magic's greatest figure, Harry Houdini.

"I did a book report on him in fourth grade, as I was interested in his escapes, but I became fascinated with the man himself," Watkins says. "He was a megalomaniac who had an obsessive ego, and he was able to be the architect of a myth about himself, a myth or legend that has persisted. One hundred years later, there is a hardly a person who has not heard of Houdini."

Watkins continued to research Houdini's life, and in 2001, he and Allen eventually put together the first version of *Death and Harry Houdini* at Chicago's Live Bait Theater. The show was much smaller than its current form, with no water torture cell, more acting and less actual magic. But the play rekindled Watkins's childhood interests. Soon, he got his magic skills back up to a point where he could start performing not as an actor but as a professional magician.

"I began working as part of the Big Apple Circus, which performed magic in hospitals for children who were ill," Watkins says. "After that, I began to get better as a magician and make some connections, so I was able to leave my other job as an administrator at the House Theater."

Death and Harry Houdini was restaged in 2003, 2012 and 2013. With more time to practice his magic and stagecraft, Watkins began to become more and more daring. It began with "smaller" tricks. During one point of the show, Watkins swallows a long black thread. After swishing it around in his mouth, there is a slight cough. Then, he pulls out the thread, but every six inches a double-edged razor blade emerges from his mouth. These demonstrations, along with card tricks, fire breathing, acrobatics and other disappearances and transformations of objects and people, all elicited gasps from audiences. Critics agreed, as the play was "highly recommend" by the *Chicago Reader*, the *Chicago Tribune*, the *Chicago Sun-Times* and most other theatrical publications. Watkins also began performing in his own one-man magic show, *The Magic Parlor*.

"We started doing it in 2010 as a fundraiser in the basement of the Chopin Theater," Watkins says. "It was a late-night, fun event that was held mostly for young people in Chicago's Wicker Park neighborhood. Then we moved to the Palmer House, and I began performing in a tuxedo at an upscale event for seventy-five dollars a ticket."

While Wicker Park is the home of the tattooed hipster, the richly paneled Empire Room and the Palmer House have seen classic entertainers from Tony Bennett and Frank Sinatra to magicians like Celeste Evans and Jay Marshall. "It is here I can perform more classic, close-up magic, as well as experiment with mentalism," Watkins says.

In his show, Watkins places silver dollars over his eyes and has an audience member duct tape them and place a blindfold over his face. Audience members write words on a board as well as hold up three objects, which Watkins names. Other tricks include producing fire from his fingertips and the razor-blade regurgitation. But it is the Chinese water torture that still wows the string of sold-out audiences.

"We started doing the water torture in 2003 at Chicago's Navy Pier," Watkins continues. "At that time, I had already gone through four years of acting, so I had improved my diaphragm, voice and musculature. It was still a lot of work practicing and practicing to hold my breath, and now I am at the point where I can do it for roughly three minutes."

Holding your breath for three minutes in your living room is one thing, but doing it upside down with your feet tied in stocks is another. Audience members at the House Theater can attest to this. Many of them try it for fun. But they aren't underwater in a claustrophobic Plexiglas tank; Watkins is. Music from the 1920s plays as cast members wander back and forth. There is a quick peek behind the black curtain. Now it has gone past two minutes, and the red hand keeps slowly moving with no sound or movement from Watkins backstage. Some in the audience begin to gasp. During many of the shows, younger children begin to become worried, and some audience members actually get up and leave. It has now been two minutes and thirty seconds. Almost everybody who was holding their breath has long since given up, and they are not soaking wet, upside down, locked in shackles. The second hand approaches two minutes and forty seconds. Where is the guy with the sledgehammer? God, I don't care if I get soaking wet or even hit with glass. That poor man is going to—Please break the damn...

Then the curtain opens. For the 200th time, Watkins stands beside the tank, gasping, dripping wet, holding onto his black goggles as the members of the crowd cheer, wipe their foreheads and remove their hands from their mouths. And they say that the Golden Age of Magic in Chicago is over?

CHAPTER 19

FUN FACTS ABOUT MAGIC

MAGICAL SONGS

For centuries, poets have used magic as a metaphor for the indescribable and unexplainable, most notably the mercurial nature of love. The creation of music, which also seems to come out of "thin air," merits strong comparisons to illusion—magician? musician?—as well. Add the psychedelic, synthesized culture of the 1960s and '70s, and the result was a slew of chart-topping hits that also played a major part in creating atmosphere for films and television shows. Here is a partial list:

"THAT OLD BLACK MAGIC," 1942. Written by the legendary team of Harold Arlen and Johnny Mercer, the song has been a standard for over eight decades. With lyrics like "That old black magic called love," it was originally recorded by Glenn Miller. Subsequent recording artists read like a who's who of popular culture during the 1940s and '50s, including Frank Sinatra, Judy Garland, Johnny Mercer, Sammy Davis Jr., Tony Bennett and Miles Davis. Perhaps the most popular version was cut by Louis Prima and Keely Smith in 1958. Marilyn Monroe also performed the song in the film *Bus Stop*, and Sinatra performed it with the altered lyrics "Old Jack Magic" for John F. Kennedy's presidential inauguration in 1961.

"THIS MAGIC MOMENT," 1960. Written by Mort Shuman and Doc Pomus, it was recorded by Ben E. King and the Drifters in 1960. Jay and the Americans scored another hit with it in 1969, as it reached #6 on the Billboard charts. A pretty straightforward song and arrangement, the song has nevertheless been covered by Lou Reed, the Misfits and the Mountain Goats.

"DO YOU BELIEVE IN MAGIC," 1965. Written by John Sebastian, this song was the first of a long string of rock hits that linked magic with music, love and occasionally psychedelic visions. Peaking at #9, it has since been used to conjure visions of the 1960s in films like *The Parent Trap*, *American Pie*, *Date Movie* and commercials for Chase Bank and McDonald's. It has been covered by Sean Cassidy and John Mellencamp, among others.

"MAGIC," 1975. Written by Dave Patton, produced by Alan Parsons and performed by the group Pilot, this song ranks alongside songs like "Brandy" as prime examples of one-hit wonders that nevertheless played a prominent role in 1970s culture. With a light psychedelic feel and lyrics, the song has continued to be a part of pop culture via its repeated use in the film *Happy Gilmore*, as well as Disney productions like *Herbie: Fully Loaded*, *Magicians* and *All Is Fair in Love*. In 2009, the tune reached another generation as it was performed by Selena Gomez for the soundtrack to the TV series *Wizards of Waverly Place*.

"STRANGE MAGIC," 1976. This song is another example of Electric Light Orchestra's unique blend of classical instruments and rock-and-roll themes. Both the introduction and bridge suggest a dreamy, mystical state. This sound helped create the ambiance of the films including *The Virgin Suicides*, *The Wizards of Waverly* and the Broadway musical version of *Xanadu*.

"MAGIC," 1980. Written by John Ferrar, the song was performed by Olivia Newton John as part of the soundtrack for the film *Xanadu*. It reached #1 on the Billboard charts in both the United States and Canada. It was the third best-selling song of 1980s compilations and was considered by many to be the only salvageable portion of a cinematic flop.

"EVERY LITTLE THING SHE DOES IS MAGIC," 1981. One of the top hits created by the Police, one of the most creative rock bands of any era, the song uses the "magic" theme in both the synthesizer of Jean Roussel and the imagery of its lyrics to create a magical vision of unattainable beauty. The song has been covered by over twenty-five artists, including John Legend, John Mayer, the Black-Eyed Peas, Ja Rule and Gloria Estefan.

"ABRACADABRA," 1982. Written by Steve Miller and performed by the Steve Miller Band, the song's bouncy keyboard riff and nonsensical lyrics personify what a pop song should be—simple, catchy and repetitive enough so that you can't get it out of your head. It hit #1 on the Billboard charts for two weeks in the United States and also topped the charts in five other countries. It has been covered by Sugar Ray and Dos Pop and was featured in the 2013 magic-inspired film *The Incredible Burt Wonderstone*.

"MAGIC," 1984. Written and sung by lead vocalist Ric Ocasek of the Cars, the tune is a straight-ahead love song, once again using the metaphor of magic to describe mystical romance. Another magical moment occurs in the video. During a party, the guests sink into a swimming pool, while Ocasek seems to stand on water—a demonstration of his love's "magic."

"Magic," 2007. Bruce Springsteen, the rock-and-roll legend who has written lyrics about fast cars, desperate love, backstreets and even the circus, tries his poetic pen with another American myth: magic. With lyrics like "I have a card up my sleeve and I'll make it disappear" or "I've got a rabbit in my hat, if you want to come and see," the Boss compares his love and desire to the force of magic. Taken from his 2007 album of the same title, it was one of the first new studio efforts with the E Street Band. Unlike many of his more stripped-down E Street efforts, "Magic" has a rich, fully produced sound. The mandolin and violin background add to Springsteen's Americana, Tom Joad persona.

"Magic," 2010. Written and performed by Colbie Caillat, this typical post–teeny bopper love song with lyrics like "you've got magic in your eyes" mines the same vein that has been tapped many times before. But with Caillat's folky guitar and breathy voice, this touch of light romance should go fine with a cup of Starbucks on the way to the mall.

"Magic," 2010. The third single from B.o.B's debut album, *B.o.B Presents, the Adventures of Bobby Ray*, "Magic" combines hip-hop and features Weezer's lead singer, Rivers Cuomo. The song, which made it up to #10 on the U.S. Billboard chart, repeats the word magic eighty-seven times. I guess he figures if he says it enough, he will become a magician.

CHAPTER 20

CELEBRITY MAGICIANS

Like magic, much that we see in film is an illusion. Or, as Francis Ford Coppola said, "I think cinema, movies and magic have always been closely associated. The very earliest people who made film were magicians."

Not only were many great directors part-time magicians, so, too, were many other celebrities and performers. Here is a partial list:

ORSON WELLES. Perhaps it comes as no surprise that the actor, radio performer, writer and director of the film that many critics still deem the greatest of all time (*Citizen Kane*) was also a magician. Neither is his boisterous claim that, while still a child, he was personally taught magic by Houdini. Nevertheless, Welles was well known around Hollywood for his performances of magic tricks at events and parties. Besides touring was a magician and performing magic for U.S. troops as part of a USO tour, Welles also appeared in the films *Follow the Boys* and *Casino Royale* as a magician. In his final years, Welles filmed an unfinished television special, *The Orson Welles Magic Show*, which was screened at the Munich Film Festival.

JOHNNY CARSON. The undisputed king of late-night television was also a fan of magic. In fact, the young Carson got his start in show business as a magician. At the age of twelve, Carson found a book of magic at a friend's house. A short time later, he purchased a magic kit and began performing at local events as the Great Carsini. While in the U.S. Navy, he performed magic for his shipmates as well as James Forrestal, secretary of the navy, on the USS *Pennsylvania*. Although he soon gave up magic for broadcasting, he was widely known for his interest in and appreciation of magic and had over thirty different magicians perform on the *Tonight Show* during its run.

Woody Allen. Allen said that as a child he was not a great athlete, so he turned to magic as a hobby, practicing tricks endlessly and saving his thirty-five-cent lunch money to buy them. "The years went by, to no avail. I never was invited to parties to perform magic," he said. "Nor could I ever get anyone to pick a card." He later found success as a magician—on film—playing the character magician Sid Waterman, aka the Great Splendini, in his 2006 film *Scoop*.

Steve Martin. Besides being an Emmy Award–winning actor, comic and Grammy Award–winning banjo player, Steve Martin was also an accomplished magician. As a teenager, he worked performing magic tricks at Disneyland. Later on, one of his major breakthroughs was his appearance on the *Tonight Show* as the Great Flydini. During this skit, Martin managed to produce lit cigarettes, a ringing phone, a martini and a singing Pavarotti puppet from his lower extremity zipper.

Jason Alexander. The *Seinfeld* star also dreamed of becoming a magician as a child. But recently, his dream came true, as in April 2013 he performed at Hollywood's Magic Castle. After his performance, he stated, "While it was a cherished fantasy of mine [to perform at the Magic Castle], the reality was laden with self-doubt and no small dose of dread. I stopped pursuing magic as a career when I was a young teen because I knew I was not good enough to stand beside the brilliant men and women I saw performing around me. I loved and respected magic too much to have it compromised by my own hand."

Neil Patrick Harris. In the article "Hollywood's Secret Magicians," writer Emily Fiemster reported that *How I Met Your Mother* star Neil Patrick Harris tried sleight of hand, having performed magic on the *Tonight Show*, starring Johnny Carson, and the *Late Show* with David Letterman. "I've been a magician for years and years and years," he said. "I don't really perform actively as much as I love studying it and watching other magicians."

On the website magictricks.com, author Jackie Morticup provided a more complete list of amateur/ celebrity magicians, including: Dick Van Dyke, Andy Griffith, Bob Barker, Muhammad Ali, Adrien Brody, Prince Charles, Don Johnson, Norman Schwarzkopf, George W. Bush, Dick Cavett, Jackie Gleason, Cary Grant, Tyrone Power, Boris Karloff, Fred Astaire, Buster Keaton, Milton Berle, Jimmy Stewart, Tallulah Bankhead, Barbara Stanwyck, Harold Lloyd, Fred Gwynne, Karl Malden, Bill Bixby, Dom DeLuise and John Denver.

Quick Guide to Chicagoland Magic, Magicians and Magical Events

American Museum of Magic
107 East Michigan Avenue, Marshall, MI
(269) 781-7570, www.americanmuseumofmagic.org

Gabe Fajuri, Potter and Potter Auctions
info@potterauctions.com
Magic memorabilia is auctioned off regularly

Walter E. King
(773) 626-2662, www.magicofthespellbinder.com
Performs spellbinding magic

Magic Chicago
Stage 773, 1225 West Belmont Avenue, Chicago, IL
(773)-327-5252, Info@MagicChicagoShow.com
Magicians perform the first Wednesday of every month

MAGIC, INC.
5082 North Lincoln Avenue, Chicago, IL
(773) 334-2855
Magic books, magic supplies, knowledgeable staff—a living museum of Chicago magic

MAGIC MAP AND OTHER GREAT CHICAGO MAGIC INFO
www.chicagomagicstudio.com

THE MAGIC PARLOR
Chicago's Palmer House, 17 East Monroe Street, Chicago, IL
(773) 769-3832, www.denniswatkins.net
Magician Dennis Watkins performs Friday nights; *Death and Harry Houdini* is often brought back by popular demand at the House Theater

SEAN MASTERSON
www.mastersonmagic.com
Performs throughout Chicagoland

O'DONOVAN'S
2100 West Irving Park Road, Chicago, IL
(773) 478-2100
Formerly Schulien's; Al James performs tableside magic every Friday

SUPERNATURAL CHICAGO
Excalibur, 632 North Dearborn Street, Chicago, IL
(800) 979-3370, www.supernaturalchicago.com
Magic in a haunted setting by necromancer Neil Tobin

BIBLIOGRAPHY

PRINT

Burger, Eugene, and David Parr. "Speak of the Devil: A Conversation about Tony Andruzzi." *Genii Magazine*, October 2000.

Burlingame, Harlin J. *Herrmann the Magician: His Life, His Secrets*. New York, 1905.

Evans, Celeste. *I Can Still See Me*. St. Petersburg, FL: Celeste Evans Magic/Sps. Publications Inc., 2011.

Kalush, William, and Larry Sloman. *The Secret Life of Houdini: The Making of America's First Superhero*. New York: Simon and Schuster, 2008.

Marshall, Alexander "Sandy." *Beating a Dead Horse: The Life and Times of Jay Marshall*. New York: Junto Publishing, 2010.

Milbourne, Christopher. *Houdini: The Untold Story*. New York: Pocket Books, 1969.

Moering, John. *The Magical Life of Marshall Brodien*. Jefferson, NC: McFarland and Co., 2007.

Silverman, Kenneth. *Houdini!!! The Career of Eric Weiss*. New York: Harper Perennial, 1997.

Steinmeyer, Jim. *The Last Greatest Magician in the World: Howard Thurston Versus Houdini and the Battles of American Wizards*. New York: Penguin Group, 2012.

Electronic Sources

"Bangs Sisters." en.wikipedia.org/wiki/Bangs_Sisters.
"Davenport Brothers." en.wikipedia.org/wiki/Davenport_brothers.
Genii, the Conjurors Magazine. www.MagicPedia.net.
"Harry Kellar." en.wikipedia.org/wiki/Harry_Kellar.
Magic and Hollywood Celebrities. www.magictricks.com.
Map of Chicago Magic. www.chicagomagicstudio.com.
www.billboard.com.

INDEX

S

Schulien, Matt 9, 40, 64, 65
Sean Masterson 104
Society of American Magicians 28, 35,
    37, 41, 45, 76, 90, 109
Steinmeyer, Jim 22
Supernatural Chicago 93, 107, 110

T

Taylor, Jeff 36
Theater, Regal 94, 106
Thompson, Johnny 43
Thurston, Harry 22
Thurston, Howard 7, 20, 23
Tobin, Neil 35, 72, 90, 92, 93, 107
Treasure Chest 55, 70, 73, 95
TV Magic Cards 9, 42, 49, 70, 73, 74,
    100

V

vaudeville 7, 14, 16, 17, 23, 25

W

Watkins, Dennis 104, 111
Western Avenue 49
WGN (TV) 68, 70, 73, 74, 77, 107
Wizzo the Wizard (Marshall Brodien)
    9, 49, 70, 72
Wonderstone, Burt "The Incredible"
    90, 116
Woodlawn Cemetery 44
World's Fair (Chicago World's Fair) 8,
    11, 13, 23, 25, 29, 36, 40

Z

Zurbano, Maritess 85

ABOUT THE AUTHOR

David Witter is a Chicago historian and author of the book *Oldest Chicago*. A native Chicagoan, he attended Louisa May Alcott School (the same grammar school as Marshall Brodien), Lane Technical High School, Columbia College (BA in writing) and Northeastern Illinois University (BA in secondary education). Also a freelance writer and photographer, he is a regular contributor to *New City* and *Fra Noi*. His work has appeared in the *Washington Post*, the *Chicago Tribune*, the *Chicago Reader*, *Living Blues*, *The Best of the Chicago Blues Annual*, the *Bay Area Music Magazine*, the *Copley News Syndicate* and Lerner Newspapers. Witter has also taught English and special education at the Chicago Public Schools for twenty years and currently teaches at Kelly High School.